# Whiteness at the Table

# Race and Education in the Twenty-First Century

**Series Editors: Kenneth J. Fasching-Varner, Louisiana State University; Roland Mitchell, Louisiana State University; and Lori Latrice Martin, Louisiana State University**

This series asks authors and editors to consider the role of race and education, addressing questions such as "how do communities and educators alike take on issues of race in meaningful and authentic ways?" and "how can education work to disrupt, resolve, and otherwise transform current racial realities?" The series pays close attention to the intersections of difference, recognizing that isolated conversations about race eclipse the dynamic nature of identity development that play out for race as it intersects with gender, sexuality, socioeconomic class, and ability. It welcomes perspectives from across the entire spectrum of education from Pre-K through advanced graduate studies, and it invites work from a variety of disciplines, including counseling, psychology, higher education, curriculum theory, curriculum and instruction, and special education.

## Titles in Series

# Whiteness at the Table

## *Antiracism, Racism, and Identity in Education*

Edited by Shannon K. McManimon,
Zachary A. Casey, and Christina Berchini

LEXINGTON BOOKS
Lanham • Boulder • New York • London

Published by Lexington Books
An imprint of The Rowman & Littlefield Publishing Group, Inc.
4501 Forbes Boulevard, Suite 200, Lanham, Maryland 20706
www.rowman.com

6 Tinworth Street, London SE11 5AL, United Kingdom

British Library Cataloguing in Publication Information Available

**Library of Congress Cataloging-in-Publication Data**

Names: McManimon, Shannon (Shannon K.), editor. | Casey, Zachary A., 1985- editor. | Berchini, Christina, editor.
Title: Whiteness at the table : antiracism, racism, and identity in education / edited by Shannon K. McManimon, Zachary A. Casey, and Christina Berchini.
Description: Lanham : Lexington Books, [2018] | Series: Race and education in the twenty-first century | Includes bibliographical references and index. | Identifiers: LCCN 2018039563 (print) | LCCN 2018056371 (ebook) | ISBN 9781498578080 (electronic) | ISBN 9781498578073 (cloth : alk. paper) | ISBN 9781498578097 (pbk. : alk. paper)
Subjects: LCSH: Discrimination in education. | Multicultural education. | Whites--Race identity. | Race awareness.
Classification: LCC LC212 (ebook) | LCC LC212 .W44 2018 (print) | DDC 370.8--dc23
LC record available at https://lccn.loc.gov/2018039563

# Contents

# Foreword

## Decoteau J. Irby

My go-to colloquialisms for calling out white strangeness and addressing white racism come in several forms. For white folks with whom I have personal relationships I use "what up with *your* people?" and "*get your people.*" In professional settings, I state something along the lines of "white people need to do their own work" or "white folks have to figure that out." I've spoken these or similar words many times—so much so that my white students, colleagues, and friends often beat me to the punch: "We've gotta get it together." I know less about what white people think and do in response to my questions and suggestions. Sometimes they nod in agreement. Others sit in silence. Some respond in quip. My concern is not so much that white people figure themselves out for the sake of doing so. Rather I recognize that white folks have overwhelming access to resources and power such that their taken-for-granted behaviors can adversely influence the lives of people who look like me. I want white people to understand what drives their own behaviors, to figure out "what up with their people."

*Whiteness at the Table* is what happens when white people take requests like mine to heart, mind, and action. The book results from the Midwest Critical Whiteness Collective's years of making sense of the promises and perils of their commitments to antiracist thinking and practice. I first learned about MCWC when Timothy Lensmire invited me to serve as a discussant for a symposium at the annual meeting of the American Educational Research Association. I accepted the invitation and as I read the papers and prepared my notes, I found myself conflicted about what exactly the collection of papers taught me about white people, race, racism, and antiracism. What is the relationship between whiteness and depression? How do white toddlers' fantasy play teach them to be racist first graders? What should I appreciate about a study that recounts and theorizes the significance of a white woman coming into racial awareness in the moment that she smelled her Black male friend? For real? How strange. Well, not really. After all, I grew up associating white people with smells too. But this study was about Black smell. What does this have do with *me*? I thought about the times I pushed my white graduate students to research *your* people. They still mostly opted to study *us*.

Critical whiteness research is not new. Although more recent, neither is racial ambivalence research. So why did reading this particular group of white people's studies of white people seem unfamiliar? After some reflection, I realized that almost every white antiracist education research device was missing. There were no antiracist professors analyzing the inadequacies of their racist white pre-service teachers or colleagues. A racially diverse (and to be sure culturally competent and antiracist) facilitation team did not lend their expertise to improving deficient white teachers. There were no written racial autobiographies to analyze or critical discourse analyses of white people talking through their mistakes while painstakingly trying not to be racist in their classroom and professional development sessions. There were no white privilege confessionals, no tears, no person of color to set evasive white person straight. There were no communications guidelines. The manuscripts were strange.

This book presents those strange papers in a final form. Although the authors acknowledge how white supremacy structures institutional and social relations, *Whiteness at the Table* pivots from the assumption that white people are deficient racial subjects who benefit wholesale from white privilege. The pivot translates into a book that presents no cases of white "antiracists" working to fix white "racists." It also eschews liberal approaches that fetishize rituals of unpacking invisible white privilege knapsacks. Rather, the authors' commitments to both antiracism and anti-essentialism yields complex portrayals of whiteness and white people's thoughts and behaviors, with an emphasis on the question of how to be white and committed to antiracism in a racist world where white supremacy morphs to fit with the changing times. It suggests that white people can be committed to antiracism while raising children who learn to be racist and that white people can live with and love racist parents and families while forging communities and identities that are race conscious. It suggests teachers can do antiracist work in their schools and experience fear and inadequacy while doing so.

Each chapter underscores the central idea that racial entrenchment and racial progress can coincide in the same time and space, be it at home, at school, or in one's thoughts and actions. Reading this book encouraged me to think more deeply about white people's responses to my "what up with your people?" questions and requests. Perhaps the silences and nods of agreement are an evasive gesture that reflects a sense of fear or loss about what to do with their brothers, sisters, mothers, fathers, spouses, children, students, colleagues, neighbors, or what to do with white strangers. Perhaps, the nods and silences signal that they "see" what I am asking them to disrupt. They know there is work to do even though how to do it remains elusive. It may be a recognition that the heavy lifting of the work is theirs to do, however uncomfortable it may be. Perhaps the silences and nods signal all the above.

Decoteau J. Irby
    University of Illinois at Chicago
    Educational Policy Studies

# Introduction

## Timothy J. Lensmire

This is a story about a small collective of people—the people who wrote and edited this book. I'll begin with a story about how we began. [1]

Once upon a time, in 2009, Audrey Lensmire thought back on her graduate school days and expressed dissatisfaction. She had wanted to take up race and the experiences of white urban teachers in her work, but had found almost no one among faculty and classmates who could help her do this. *faculty advisors* Those who did help were people she didn't know, people she knew only through their writing and theorizing, such as the philosopher Charles Mills and the Reverend Thandeka.

I had been telling Audrey about some graduate students at the University of Minnesota—Mary Lee-Nichols, Jessie Dockter Tierney, Shannon McManimon, Zac Casey—a rather incredible collection of educators and activists interested in race and whiteness. None of them were playing at this: they had, for years, been breaking their heads and backs on the problem of how to mobilize white people for antiracism and social justice. Included in my enthusiasm was Bryan Davis, a graduate student in educational administration at the University of Wisconsin-Milwaukee. I had been corresponding with Bryan about research he wanted to do on how white high school principals made sense of race and racism.

That is when Audrey—rather than simply allowing me to enjoy the fact that I knew these beautiful people—told me in some detail and with increasing anger about how dissatisfied she had been with her graduate school experience.

She said that we should start a group.

We did.

The Midwest Critical Whiteness Collective was born.

\*\*\*

There is a second way that our collective (I'll call it MCWC from now on) was born of *dissatisfaction*. However, to persist in this theme feels like perversion, for MCWC has been quite the opposite of dissatisfying.

A few years after we began, Sam Tanner, and then Christina Berchini, joined us—joined this collective committed to telling difficult and complex stories, committed to making sense of these stories in multiple and powerful ways. Over time, MCWC became a place of hard and satisfying intellectual work, as well as a place of hard and tears-in-your-eyes laughter—at our own ridiculousness, at the world's absurdities. Our meetings take place at Audrey's and my dining room table, and for its members, MCWC became (and remains) a place of sustenance, one that inspires courage, a place of deepening regard and love.

A second way MCWC was born of dissatisfaction is that all of us, even before we assembled, had grown frustrated with the current dominant critical framework in the United States for understanding whiteness and pursuing antiracism in education—a *white privilege* framework popularized by writers such as Peggy McIntosh and Tim Wise. Our dissatisfaction was mostly inarticulate, felt more than thought-through. As was our custom, we started telling each other stories—stories about our experiences as participants in, and leaders of, antiracist efforts grounded in this framework's assumptions. As was our custom, we tried to figure out what these stories meant. Soon enough, we decided that we needed to go back and read, carefully, vigorously, one of the founding texts of this perspective, McIntosh's (1988) "White privilege and male privilege: A personal account of coming to see correspondences through work in women's studies."

From the beginning, MCWC's main purpose was to provide support for members who were always already engaged in all sorts of antiracist work with other people and in other spaces. But when we gathered around McIntosh's essay, we realized that we wanted to take up a project together, as a collective. Drawing on our stories and our critical readings of McIntosh, we put together a presentation to share at a conference on critical whiteness studies at the University of Iowa and then at the American Educational Research Association's annual meeting in Vancouver, British Columbia.

The work of creating this presentation (which was eventually published as an article in *Harvard Educational Review*), as well as the responses of audiences to our work, taught us much. We learned to articulate some of our dissatisfactions with this critical framework focused on white privilege—that it misunderstands white privilege as cause rather than effect of a white supremacist society; that it ignores complexities and conflicts that attend learning to be and being white, with dire consequences for imagining antiracist work with white people; and that the pedagogy born of this framework too often results in little more than tears and confessions of white privilege from the "good" white people and resistance from the "bad."

Our audiences surprised us. We were expecting more opposition from true believers invested in this framework's theory and practice. Instead, there were polite questions in public, followed by rich, searching conversations around the edges of official conference spaces. Maybe this is not so out of the ordinary, but what felt different was that, whether or not the conversations were whispered (some were), *these conversations felt like they were being whispered.* These were underground exchanges. What became clear was, first, that it somehow felt dangerous for people—people of color, white people—to make open criticisms of white privilege work (probably because they understood that such criticisms might be used by others to mark them as regressive or racist); and second, that they had their own criticisms of this framework and had been toiling in their own teaching and activism to work through or around its limitations.

All that said, you should know that when we gather around the dining room table and reminisce about this early work with McIntosh's ideas, what we talk about most is that we didn't know how to pronounce *the* key word in the title of our presentation. There we were, at the University of Iowa, with our presentation all carefully planned out, and we didn't know how to say "synecdoche."

Our central claim and insight was that McIntosh's work on white privilege acted as a synecdoche, as a stand in, for all the antiracist work to be done, and that this limited our understanding of whiteness and our ability to imagine possibilities for antiracist action. But we didn't know how to say "synecdoche." Zac found an audio pronunciation online and played it for us, over and over. And we must have said the word out loud hundreds of times in Iowa City, first in nervous anticipation of our presentation and then, afterward, for laughs, as we confessed to almost everyone we talked to at the conference that we hadn't known how to pronounce the word.

\*\*\*

I draw three morals from this story of McIntosh-as-synecdoche, whispered criticisms, and using a word we couldn't pronounce.

The first is that, as a collective, we get out ahead of ourselves sometimes (you can treat our inability to pronounce "synecdoche" as a synecdoche for this tendency). However, we have learned to embrace this, not only as *unavoidable* when trying to figure out difficult things, but as *good*. We have learned to trust leaps forward, intuitions, felt senses of things—have learned to trust them at least long enough to see if there is anything important there. Obviously, leaps and intuitions do not always turn out to be right or fruitful. This is one of the reasons that laughter and affection are so crucial to our collective, because they help us survive being wrong and looking silly. Another way of saying this is that we have learned to trust stories, emotions, our bodies—and that this trust is coupled to a commitment to the hard labor of catching up to and interpreting what our bodies and stories already know and express.

The second moral of this story is that we are dedicated to mobilizing theory and history in our work. We engage these not for their own sake, nor for the purpose of fooling ourselves or others that we are smarter than we are. Instead, we are compelled by history and theory (and fancy words such as "synecdoche") because they do work for us—because they help us understand or name things powerfully, because they open up possibilities for action.

Our intellectual debts are many and varied, as will be made plain in the chapters that follow. I hesitate to reduce this multiplicity, here, but draw on the different ways that Robyn Wiegman (1999) and Troy Duster (2001) break down scholarship on whiteness, in order to characterize how we orient ourselves in our work.

In her appraisal of the field of critical whiteness studies, Wiegman (1999) identified three "schools" that represented different "trajectories of inquiry": the race traitor school, the white trash school, and the class solidarity school. For MCWC, the writings of labor historians and cultural critics in Wiegman's third school—which she reads as attempting to rethink the "history of working-class struggle as the preamble to forging new cross-racial alliances" (p. 121)—have been foundational. Wiegman points to historian David Roediger's (1991) *Wages of Whiteness* as initiating the modern study of whiteness. Roediger, for his part, would brush aside this suggestion and direct our attention, instead, to W. E. B. Du Bois's (1935/1992) *Black Reconstruction in America, 1860-1880*—and especially Du Bois's notion of a "psychological wage" paid to white workers, so they aligned themselves with white elites rather than their Black sisters and brothers—as a more suitable place to start the story. In living out our engagement with this line of inquiry, we have assumed, with Roediger (1998), that writers of color have often been "the nation's keenest students of white consciousness and white behavior" (p. 4).

For Duster (2001), scholarship on whiteness can be divided into two "sharply conflicting" perspectives: one that portrays whiteness as fluid, contingent, and relational, and another that emphasizes the "deeply embedded, structural, hard, enduring, solid-state features of race and racism" (p. 113). Duster argues, in the end, that we need *both* these ways of conceiving whiteness, but he also believes that the "study of whiteness as a relationship" is likely the "most promising" of future work in this area (p. 131). Our book emphasizes, in the main, situated and relational aspects of whiteness—our title, *Whiteness at the Table*, is meant to suggest this. That said, we also attend to enduring and structural aspects of white supremacy. The challenge, as Maurice Berger (1999) noted, is "how to advocate the idea of whiteness as a useful classification for examining white power and prestige without ignoring its limitation in defining and describing its subjects" (p. 206).

The third and final moral to this story, then, is that so much more is needed—for conceptualizing white people as racialized actors in U.S. society, for imagining and pursuing antiracism in education—than what a white privilege framework is able to provide. Advocates of this framework have been trying to use, in Duster's terms, a "solid-state" conception of whiteness to inform, somehow, the unavoidably messy and relational task of white people re-making their hearts and minds. Or, as James Jupp and Patrick Slattery (2010) put it: "What a tragic error . . . to emphasize essentializing stasis, if that is what, in fact, we seek to change" (p. 471).

*[handwritten margin note: what white privilege frame omits]*

\*\*\*

Audrey's synagogue in Minneapolis, Shir Tikvah, includes a fair number of interfaith couples and families. Shir Tikvah's warm, playful designation for non-Jews like me is *Jew-adjacent*. So I will call the author of our first chapter, Erin Miller (a Southerner, of all things, and professor at the University of North Carolina-Charlotte), *MCWC-adjacent*, given all the work and writing she has done with us over the years, given all the mutual respect and affection.

Erin's chapter is the first of three that hone in on how whiteness is constructed within families and local communities. Erin's crucial contributions to *Whiteness at the Table* include her close examination of how young children (her own) learn to be white, and how this learning is, in turn, wrapped up tightly with learning to be Christian, middle class, and patriotic.

*[handwritten margin note: Erin Miller]*

Sam and Audrey's chapter also focuses on being young and learning to be white, but the stories, here, come from their own childhoods—specifically, Audrey and Sam explore their relationships with their fathers, who both suffered with serious mental health issues. The inspiration for their chapter actually came from one of Sam's high school students who, in her own attempt to figure out what being white meant, had proposed that *whiteness* and *depression* might be related in ways that needed to be investigated.

Christina also narrates stories from her own life in her chapter, but in these stories, she is older than Erin's children, older than Audrey and Sam were, when they were learning to be white with their fathers. She may be older (her stories commence as she nears the completion of her PhD), but Christina is still her mother's daughter. It is this relationship—its complexities, its clashes, its silences—that Christina centers as she works through what it means to be a white, antiracist daughter who loves her white, sometimes skeptical mother.

*First 3 chapters → family*

*Final 3 chapters → school*

***

The final three chapters of our book emphasize school more than family (though the boundaries of these always and everywhere blur). At the heart of Mary and Jessie's chapter about white rural teachers and our nation's color-blind ideology is an enigma: what are we to make of white teachers who claim to *literally* not see race? In their attempt to solve this puzzle, Jessie and Mary provide a clear demonstration of why structural and "solid-state" accounts of race and racism are inadequate for understanding how whiteness and white racial identities are lived out and pursued within specific local contexts and relationships.

The relationships at stake in Bryan's and my chapter are small and big. Our chapter is about a relationship between two high school teenagers, one of whom grows up to be a high school principal. It is about how this white woman principal positions herself in relation to various and conflicting discourses about race, as she tells about a time that she took a drive in a car with her Black high school friend, Bob. And it is about how white patriarchal fears that white women will have sex with Black men direct this white principal to keep her distance from Black students and their families.

*Ch. 6*

The white women teachers featured in Zac and Shannon's chapter do *not* keep their distance from students of color, nor from tackling problems of racism in their schools. They are doing serious, concrete, antiracist work in their classrooms and buildings. At the same time, they are fearful that their antiracist work might harm relationships with colleagues, they are worried that they might somehow do antiracism wrong, and they are deeply troubled that they will never be able to do enough.

*"studying up"*

Antiracist work in education has proceeded as if the only social relation at issue is the one between white people and people of color. Obviously, this is the relationship with which we should, in the end, be most concerned. But what if our antiracist efforts are being undermined by unexamined difficulties and struggles *among white people*?

*TITLE of Book*

Our book's title is *Whiteness at the Table*, then, for at least three reasons. First, it is meant to evoke the origins of this book, to conjure the image and sound of MCWC telling and interpreting stories at Audrey's and my dining room table. Second, our book's title emphasizes that we are theorizing whiteness not just in terms of structural aspects of white power, but in terms of how whiteness is worked out, reproduced, challenged, in day-to-day interactions and relationships among white children, youth, and adults. In this sense, whiteness is always already *at the table*, and our book seeks to illuminate how and why this is so. Finally, our title is meant to suggest a moral and political demand that white people *bring whiteness*—as an explicit topic, as perhaps the most important problem to be solved at this historical moment—*to the table*.

*these are the spaces I know most about and feel most capable of dismantling*

It is not right that this responsibility to theorize and combat whiteness fall only to people of color. Thus, Shannon and Zac's final chapter is an appropriate one to close our book, not only for its portrayal of white people doing significant antiracist work with each other, but also because it reminds us— as do all our chapters—that relationships among white people determine, to a profound extent, how white people orient themselves toward people of color.

\*\*\*

Five years after our first conference presentation together, MCWC put together another one. This time, we knew how to pronounce all of the important words and we invited two of our favorite scholars—Beverly Cross and Decoteau Irby—to provide critical responses to our work. We knew Decoteau because of a devastating piece he had written on the draconian disciplinary regime currently confronting Black male youth in our schools. And Beverly is something of a hero to us, if for no other reason than because she wrote one of the fiercest and most illuminating critiques of mainstream teacher education reform that we have.

That presentation, in Chicago, was the earliest draft of this book. We are grateful that Beverly and Decoteau joined us for that presentation, and grateful that they've written the first and last words of our book. We are glad that they are *MCWC-adjacent*.

\*\*\*

I could say that there is a third way that MCWC was born of *dissatisfaction*—our dissatisfaction with a white supremacist U.S. society and its schools. But this would be incorrect. "Dissatisfaction" was appropriate for expressing Audrey's wish that she could have worked at understanding and combatting racism, in graduate school, in communion with others; and the word was apt for positioning us in relation to McIntosh and Wise's white privilege framework. In relation to white supremacy? Better words (though still inadequate) would be disgust and outrage.

This is a book about whiteness, written (except for Decoteau and Beverly) by white people. With all my talk of MCWC's laughter and warmth, and with all the attention paid, in the chapters that follow, to the complexities and costs of whiteness for white people, perhaps this all seems a bit soft on racism.

We condemn white supremacy, condemn all the horrific and mundane violences perpetrated by white people, against people of color, as part of keeping the system going. We attempt to revise how whiteness and white racial identities are conceived, in *Whiteness at the Table*, exactly because we believe that this will support the development of more effective and powerful

How can *white* youth in #USvsHate make critical public-facing messages that bring whiteness to the table?

pedagogies—ones that actually engage and mobilize white people for antiracist action.

## REFERENCES

Berger, M. (1999). *White lies: Race and the myths of whiteness.* New York: Farrar, Straus & Giroux.

Du Bois, W. E. B. (1992/1935). *Black reconstruction in America, 1860-1880.* New York: The Free Press.

Duster, T. (2001). The "morphing" properties of whiteness. In B. Rasmussen, E. Klinenberg, I. Nexica, & M. Wray (Eds.), *The making and unmaking of whiteness* (pp. 113-137). Durham & London: Duke University Press.

Jupp, J., & Slattery, P. (2010). Committed white male teachers and identifications: Toward creative identifications and a "Second Wave" of white identity studies. *Curriculum Inquiry, 40*(3), 454–474.

McIntosh, P. (1988). White privilege and male privilege: A personal account of coming to see correspondences through work in women's studies (Working Paper 189). Wellesley, MA: Wellesley Center for Research on Women.

Roediger, D. (1991). *The wages of whiteness.* London: Verso.

Roediger, D. (Ed.). (1998). *Black on white: Black writers on what it means to be white.* New York: Random House.

Wiegman, R. (1999). Whiteness studies and the paradox of particularity. *Boundary 2, 26*(3), 115–50.

## NOTES

1. Beginnings, of course, can always be pushed further back or forward in time. The author chooses where to start, and may or may not (depending on the genre of the piece, depending on the author's awareness and ideological commitments), remind the reader about this choosing, its arbitrariness, its inevitability.

# Chapter One

# Race, Class, Patriotism, and Religion in Early Childhood: The Formation of Whiteness

### Erin T. Miller

*keywords*
*(construction of) children's white racial identity, ethnography, whiteness, mostly white community*

> Max (five-year-old white child): Did you know that our church is doing a really good thing? They are giving money to poor people.
> Author (mother): What poor people?
> Max: They are the Indians. . . They live in Africa.

*early childhood; 9 month ethnography*

This vignette, collected from a nine-month critical ethnography investigating race and racism in early childhood contexts and described in this chapter, tells a story of the construction of children's white racial identity mediated by class, religion, colonialism, and patriotism. A critical way to study racism is to challenge the dominant, typically unexamined, view of whiteness and thus, in referring to whiteness, I refer to the *implicit normalizations of the oppression of persons of color by white people as manifested globally, nationally, and locally.* I believe that recognizing how racism is taught and learned in the worlds of young white children offers insights into how inequities are perpetuated in our U.S. society.

*DEFINE whiteness*

   The stories described here, all part of a larger ethnography, were generated from the lived experiences of my three young children: Ella (9 years old), Olivia (6 and 7 years old), and Max (5 years old). I chose to study my own children because (a) at the time of the study, they fell within or near the U.S. National Association for the Education of Young Children (NAEYC)'s definition of what it means to be a young child in the United States (children from birth through age eight), (b) they self-identified as being white, and (c) we lived in and thus, they were growing up in, a mostly white community. I concentrated on my own children, rather than on other children, because of

*studying her own white children in a mostly white community*

*what are other phrases folks use? "predominantly white spaces"? look up*

*[handwritten margin note: Why study her own kids]*

the perspectives I had as a mother on learning and growth and because of the opportunities I had to collect data ethnographically in the daily contexts of their lives. I had access to unfiltered, intimate, familial moments that would be difficult for an outsider to obtain. I continuously drew inspiration in terms of the advantages of my role from other parent researchers (Bissex, 1980; Butler, 1980; Long, 2004; Martens, 1996) whose positions as insiders in the worlds of their children profoundly strengthened the knowledge base in their respective fields of study.

## STORIES OF BECOMING WHITE

*[handwritten margin note: in 9 months, only 10 explicitly racial convos, BUT ✳]*

I collected stories from my children for approximately nine months to better understand how they were becoming white in our home and community contexts; in all of that time, I captured less than ten explicit, in-depth conversations about race. Yet, as I began to analyze data, I realized that it was not necessary for my children to have explicit conversations about race and the social implications of racial difference for them to receive, construct, deconstruct, and/or interrupt racialized messages. The stories told here demonstrate how, in the lives of my children, messages of whiteness as the norm were prolific yet difficult to notice because they were disguised as normal. They were, in essence, so interwoven into the backdrop of our lives that they were easily indistinguishable to the untrained eye. As a parent, I also experienced our interactions as a normal part of our day-to-day existence, and my own sense of white racial identity both implicitly and explicitly shaped how I engaged in this research as a mother. In fact, training our white eyes to become aware of racial hegemony became an important part of this study and something I discuss in detail in other work (Miller, 2015; Miller, 2016; Miller, 2017). In what follows, I focus on the larger social structure of my children's social lives, including their interactions with me, as a way of understanding the hegemonic character of whiteness and white racial identity. Because of my focus on understanding whiteness as it was being constructed, I do not detail interventions, but instead I work to privilege the voices and experiences of my children through the lens of a researcher.

Through an analysis of these stories, I found that learning to be white did not happen in isolation from learning other identities—learning to be middle class; learning to be Christian; learning to navigate contradictory and competing discourses about humankind, U.S. nationalism, and pluralism. These identities were also intertwined in the process of learning to be raced. This all led to a deeper level of complexity regarding racial identity formation. Some studies that examine children's (and adults') understanding of race posit that human beings move through racialized phases or developmental time periods (Aboud, 2003; Brown, 2010; Van Avermaet & McClintock, 1988); however,

*[handwritten margin note: intersections]*

in this nine-month study, I found nothing linear or isolated about the process of learning to be raced in my children's lives. The dominant discourses that shaped three young white children's construction of race, particularly what it means to be white, were multi-faceted, contradictory, and completely mixed up with learning about and learning how to navigate a world composed of multiple identity narratives. Trying to make sense of this as a researcher *and* as a parent only added to this complexity.

## WHITENESS "IN THE MIDDLE"

For Ella, Olivia, and Max, learning to be white happened concurrently with learning to identify themselves as middle class. Defining what it means to be middle class is complex, disputable, broadly theorized, and narrowly re-searched (Lareau & Conley, 2008), at times encompassing and at times ex-cluding socioeconomic indexes, education, and occupation. Yet, most agree that social class is, at the very least, a manifestation of social hierarchy. My children indicated that they understood class as representing either poor, middle, or rich, but becoming classed and becoming raced were intricately linked. The fact that most of the events in *their* middle-class lives were dominated by white people meant that they received strong messages that the class structures in which their worlds revolved were the territory of whites. In our broader geographic context (Columbia, South Carolina) and in the small-er contexts within my children's lives in particular (shopping facilities, schools, children's sports facilities, dance studios, our church, etc.), econom-ic privilege has been historically and is today disproportionately experienced by whites and the largely segregated class lines are marked by race. As such, my family's middle-class identity marker is contextualized within a racist social and historical framework (Morris & Monroe, 2009). In South Caroli-na, little progress has been made in widening the racial demographics of the middle class, who remain mostly white. For example African-American men and women hold one-third of all state jobs, yet they are over-represented in low-wage state positions—nearly two-thirds of African Americans in South Carolina earn less than $21,000 per year. What this means for my children's construction of whiteness is that they learned, by experience and observation, not necessarily explicit conversation, that they are a part of a particular context characterized by particular activities and particular norms largely made up of white actors. Therefore, implicit messages about who belongs and who does not belong in their lives were taught through their participation in normalized daily life.

Clearly, this distancing of white and Black lives played a critical role in my children's understanding of middle class-ness as white. Segregated spaces, created by racist ideologies and practices and reinforced by economic discrepancies, provide fertile ground for white children to associate what is normal with what they see white people doing, leading to a larger normalization of white culture. In the following sections, I tell stories to support the argument that, in Ella, Olivia, and Max's day-to-day activities, many messages reinforced middle class as normal *and* as the domain of whiteness. The specific messages that my children received and seemed to internalize are described in the following sections where I discuss links between class and race that were salient in their/our worlds.

## White Boundaries: Middle-Class Neighborhoods

The places in which we reside, shop, entertain, go to school, engage in extracurriculars, and so on, have often been seen as powerful indicators of class and serve as a segregating tool for race (Freund, 2007). For Ella, Olivia, and Max, racialized experiences reinforced that our "places" were codified by whiteness. This was blatantly clear one day when I took Ella and her best friend and neighbor Christine on an outing to celebrate Ella's tenth birthday. In the car, the girls spontaneously began to talk about memories they shared as neighbors and friends, including times when groups of African-American boys came to *their* white dominant neighborhood from the adjacent African-American neighborhood of low-income, single-dwelling houses and a large public housing project named Gonzales Gardens. The physical boundary between these two neighborhoods is a street—Manning Street—but the social boundaries are the constructed-to-be-impenetrable borders of race and class difference.

The girls recounted memories of a time when these boundaries were broken within a discourse of fear and racial hegemony, reinforced by their recollection of the reactions of neighborhood parents. Christine described a time when she witnessed a group of African-American boys take a baseball bat from a white neighbor's yard:

> I was in my house. I was going outside to see what Ella [was doing] and if she was home or not and so I saw these boys coming. I was like, "Mom, some boys stole [a white neighbor's] baseball bat" and she was like "What?" She found the boys and I don't know exactly what she said but she was like talking to 'em. Then this big boy, a big brother, came out and so he was being all nice at first. And then the big brother got mad at her, at my mom, and they started insulting her and then my dad just got out of the bathroom and he came out and he's like, and he said something about, like, I *think* he said I'm going to go, I'm going to take you out down the river and drown you. And, because he wasn't— he wasn't trying to be mean; he was just trying to make them stop and get out of our neighborhood.

This example demonstrates how class identifications, largely developed through neighborhood affiliation, were codified by race and racial boundaries. While the geographical, cultural, and racial landscape of our world permits "white world travelers" (Sullivan, 2004) to move in and out of Black spaces, Black people, in the white imaginary, are expected to adhere to the rigid boundaries most often and blatantly created by wealth distribution. The boys in this story were from a Black, low-income neighborhood characterized by poverty (dilapidated, congested apartment buildings on a bulldozed lot with no trees where residents share clothes lines in a communal yard), and they entered into a white, middle-class space characterized by wealth (wide streets, landscaped yards, sweeping "historic" and preserved trees, and large, single family homes) and allegedly stole a baseball bat and insulted a white woman. The result was that the boys' *lives* were threatened when the white woman's white husband, perhaps as a self-imaged act of valiance, threatened, "I'm going to take you down to the river." The imagery is haunting when we consider the thousands of Black men across the South who were murdered and whose bodies were thrown into rivers in the long-reaching history of racism in the United States. For example, evoking the 1898 Wilmington, North Carolina, massacre, white segregationist Leroy Gibson threatened a crowd in the 1970s that if integration did not end in North Carolina, "we're gonna clog that river with dead niggers" (Tyson, 2005, p. 275). Given this historical context and the *consistency* of white men killing Black men in the proclaimed defense of white women and throwing their Black bodies into rivers, this incident speaks to a reality of racial terror that cannot be understated.

Ella and Christine, witnessing this interaction and later recounting it, learned a powerful lesson on whiteness as well as white femininity, both anchored in class boundaries marked by distinctly different, yet adjacent neighborhoods. The lesson went something like this: spaces are disaggregated by wealth and poverty wherein wealth is occupied by white actors and poverty is occupied by Black actors. Physically crossing those boundaries is wrong for people of color, although white people can, at times, cross into Black spaces in the name of charity (e.g., dropping off used items at the Salvation Army in the Black neighborhood), but the *worst* thing a Black boy can do is cross into a wealthy/white boundary and insult a white woman. Although the girls may not have known this, they nevertheless understood that what the boys did was culturally viewed as wrong by Christine's family, and thus, they justified the father's response by defending his actions and promoting his efforts to retain racial hegemony by putting everyone involved back into their wealthy/white and poverty/Black spaces: "he wasn't—he wasn't trying to be mean; he was just trying to make them stop and get out of our neighborhood."

The girls may not yet have understood that when white people perceive Black men as acting aggressively toward white women, it taps into what Deliovsky (2010) theorizes as the biggest fear of white men: that Black men will have sex with white women and "taint" the white race, resulting in a white male loss of power and white property. When the girls witnessed this interaction, they were faced with a dilemma. Perhaps they were uneasy with the violent racism at play but, at ten years old, they had two choices as they told this story: to name the injustice as they (and if they) understood it and risk what they may have perceived to be consequences of this, such as being disavowed/punished/corrected by their white families, or act in the way of loyalty toward their white families. The girls chose the second option and enacted what Deliovsky calls a performance of normative white femininity wherein they committed to racial and sexual loyalty by siding with and defending the white father, acting in ways that Moon (1999) describes as "good (white) girls" (p. 195). If the story itself is an account of racial femininity, the impetus for the story—the crossing of boundaries by the Black boys—was the social division of the classed neighborhoods themselves.

At this point in my recounting of this narrative, it is important to spend a little time reflecting on my role as a white parent witnessing this conversation between Ella and Christine. Part of my methodology in this study was to use data collection tools that were normalized in the environment of our lives. I often used my cell phone to record conversations my children had in the car and while they knew I was recording at all times, they were so familiar with the phone recording them that they often forgot they were being recorded. This felt important to me as an ethnographer—I wanted the children's conversations to be as authentic as possible even if the content of their conversation was troubling to me. During this particular conversation, the girls had forgotten about the recorder and largely forgotten I was listening to them. I did not interrupt this story to teach the children antiracist lessons as a counternarrative. This is not to say that I never did so during the course of the study. But, in their telling of this particular story, I felt that my interruption would temper their narration, perhaps indicate that the children were talking about something they weren't supposed to, and I felt I would lose their trust as a researcher. I danced this dance during the study for the entire nine months I collected stories—when should I jump in and intervene? When should I simply collect data no matter how raw and racist it was? I often made these decisions moment-by-moment rather than operating on an established template.

## White People as Financially "in the Middle"

It seemed clear that my children were aware of being middle class in our economically stratified society. Knowing themselves as financially middle class went hand-in-hand with knowing themselves as white and vice versa. Several times during the study, they revealed their certainty that we were middle class. Although not naming themselves as classed, they felt sure that we were not poor and not rich. For example, a discussion of being poor as related to basic necessities such as food occurred during bath time one evening. Max and Olivia launched into a song they learned through church, sung regularly after the offering:

> Give thanks with a grateful heart.
> Give thanks to the Holy One.
> For He's given Jesus Christ His Son.
> And now let the weak say I am strong.
> Let the poor say I am rich because of what the Lord has done for us.

Observing Olivia and Max singing, I asked what the hymn meant to them. I asked, "What does it mean to be grateful? Who are the poor?" Max responded by laughing, saying that we were poor. The following conversation ensued:

> Olivia: Max, we have money. (laughs)
> Max: I thought we didn't have money!
> Author (mother): No, how come we, you think we have money?
> Max: Because we could pay for something!
> Olivia: No, it means like so that like so we can go the store and buy stuff. Poor, poor people who don't have any money and who can't buy stuff.

In this and other conversations, Max and Olivia identified themselves as distinct from those who are poor. Our family has money for food and therefore we are not poor. Being poor was a domain of people of color for my children and therefore, being white was a domain of not being poor or of being middle class. For example, one night when I was giving Max a bath, he said, "Did you know that our church is doing a really good thing? They are giving money to poor people." I asked Max who poor people were and Max told me, "They are the Indians!" He later explained that "they live in Africa" and categorized people of color across countries, continents, and peoples—El Salvador, Africa, South America, and American Indians—as poor, distancing them geographically from himself. This distancing of whiteness and Blackness emerged over and over again in the stories I collected.

While Max and Olivia identified themselves as being distinct from the poor because they saw our family as having money to "buy stuff," Ella, a prolific storywriter during the time of the study, revealed, through her writing, attempts to separate herself from the upper class. She did this as she situated the protagonists and antagonists in her stories within particular class structures using economic/class markers to describe characters. For example, she often introduced her readers to a new character by writing, "Once, a little rich girl." Her disdain for and attempt to distance herself from the "rich" class were evident as the theme of bullies occurred repeatedly in her stories. The bullies were nearly always described as rich, white people. In a story that Ella wrote about bullying in the early spring of 2012, she began her narrative with: "Rich. That's the word that goes around in my head. Ok, I have to say if your rich and your reading this… BEAT IT!!!! all right. Ok now back to my story. I hate the rich." Ella's disdain for and disconnection from the upper class were exacerbated by her reading of *The Hunger Games* (Collins, 2008), a trilogy that describes a heroine who successfully brings economically oppressed districts of people together in a shared mission to overthrow a ruling class defined by opulence. Following her reading of that book, Ella developed a story of her own connecting the rich to bullying as she wrote, "OK, so there are these mean rich people called well the rulers basically and if you are caught abusing them they put you in this arena."

Locating themselves away from poor *or* rich people seemed to be a clear effort through which Ella, Olivia, and Max intentionally normalized their own lived experiences by placing themselves "in the middle" (Ella Miller, personal communication February 20, 2012). Since being in the financial middle was an experience shared by a nearly exclusive cast of white actors in their social worlds, whiteness became the only frame of reference they knew for folks who were neither poor nor rich but in the middle. Also important to note is that middle class-ness was a safely "neutral" place to be because, according to Ella's narratives and the narratives from which she drew, she was not the oppressor; the rich elite was. While some would argue lower and middle classes are indeed oppressed by the rich, the antagonistic views taken on the rich distracted Ella from paying attention to her own structural advantages that privileged her as white and middle class.

## White People Have What They Have Because of God and Hard Work

These stories led me to construct what seemed to be two competing acquisition discourses—competing bodies of thought in my children's lives that are reflected in the larger world and that struggle in the fight for power to transform society (Foucault, 1972). Obfuscating simple notions of class hierarchy and racial privileging, one discourse centered on the prevailing myth of meritocracy (McNamee & Miller, 2009) or the idea that with hard work, anyone can achieve greater economic status and thus, entrée to the middle class. The other discourse came from the children's interactions within the Christian contexts of our lives as they learned that we come to good things because of God—good things that place us firmly in the realm of the white middle class.

## Learning the Meritocracy Myth

Illustrating Olivia, Ella, and Max's growing beliefs in the meritocracy myth are data that indicate their views that doing well in life is inextricably linked to doing well in school. For example, Ella explained to Olivia and Max one afternoon while we were riding in the car: "If you wanna get a good job, you gotta do good in school." Ella continued, "So you can go to middle school and then high school. And if you do good in high school, you go to college and learn and learn what you want to do with your life. Like, if you want to be a veterinarian or a teacher, you learn how to be a teacher." It seemed clear that nothing in my children's lives had prepared them to bring issues of race and class privilege into their discussions of how one gets ahead in life. Their middle class worlds taught them well the meritocracy myth.

## God Gives

At the same time, another dominant and contradictory theme was that God gives us what we have—both material items and our gifts. A popular song we all sang during car rides was "Blessed be Your Name" (Redmond, 2005). The refrain includes a repeated message that interpreted Biblical scripture by referencing Job 1:21 (King James Version): "Naked came I out of my mother's womb, and naked shall I return thither: the Lord gave, and the Lord hath taken away; blessed be the name of the Lord." This is one of many examples of texts embedded in the children's church-based experiences that sent the message that God gives. This included daily rituals in our home. For example, nearly every night before they ate their supper, I told the children, "Put your napkin in your lap and thank God for your food."

These patterns led me to a further finding that explains a missing piece in understanding children's construction of being raced: living in middle-class, white worlds, my children constructed notions of success and of obtaining material advantages as connected to God and hard work, but never to issues of racial privilege. In other words, while they came to understand material advantages in either the stories of acquisition (God given) or achievement (rewards for hard work), there was little space for or access to opportunities to understand how race is a socially created and socially maintained marker of oppression that places barriers on attempts to attain material wealth. There was no place in which they were encouraged to ask questions such as: "If God gives to us, why not to others?" or "Does everyone who works hard actually get ahead? Why? Why not?" Furthermore, the discourses themselves are inherently contradictory: the children learned on one hand that God gives us what we have, but they also learned that hard work leads to attaining success and material wealth, and neither was connected to issues of socially constructed notions of class or race. As I came to notice these patterns through analysis, I did a better job of teaching lessons of race, racism, and antiracism when misconceptions were exposed. But again, I must reiterate that my study was designed to understand how my children were being racially socialized, even if my findings were painful truths. Thus, the focus of my study was on my children, rather than my own interventions as a parent.

## WHITENESS INTERSECTED WITH CHRISTIANITY AT KENNEDY STREET METHODIST

Despite the fact that the children most commonly interacted with others in spaces dominated by white actors, they were not without lessons of the Other. Those lessons about the Other came largely through church-related contexts, theological lessons through which race was further erased/raced out by another important identity marker—our Christian faith as learned through our church. Before describing these lessons, I remind readers that *at the time these stories were collected,* I had not yet made full sense of their practical racial implications. My goal during the time of collection was mostly to learn from my children's day-to-day lives how they were being indoctrinated into whiteness through routine interactions. As such, I did not intervene to do things like find a different church even as the dawn of the realization of how dominant whiteness was in our faith-based practices began to rise. Those interventions did occur in years to come in the aftermath of the study as I tried to make sense of the racial debris it had stirred. In the years after these stories were collected, in the years when I began to make sense of and tell the stories here, the children and I eventually left our church and tried, unsuccessfully to this date, to find an alternate faith-based home where whiteness did not reign.

### God, Biology, and Race: God Made Us and God Made Us Different

One of the most powerful messages that the children learned at church, and that was reinforced in our home, was the idea that we are a creation of God. The idea that God made us and that He made the whole world, was pervasive and insistent. Part and parcel of the message of divine creation was the idea that God made human beings different from each other, including racial differences. The children believed and taught each other that race is determined by God. For example, one night during a pilot study, Max (aged four at the time) confidently asserted, "God made you white. God made me white. And God made Ella white and Livie white because we are a white family." Max rationalized that his friend Miles was not white because God made him that way: "And God made Miles Black because he is in a Black family."

On another occasion, the children spontaneously began a game at the dinner table in which Olivia and Max listed things that God may have made and things that people were responsible for making. Ella was positioned as the teacher during this exchange, and she either affirmed or disaffirmed God's role in the creation of the suggested items:

> Max: God made our skin. God made our skin.
> Ella: I know. God made everything.
> Olivia: Except the laundry.
> Olivia: He made our cats.
> Ella: Uh-huh.
> Olivia: He made the grass.
> Ella: No, someone invented grass.

As the game continued, Ella confirmed for Olivia and Max that all of our physical characteristics (e.g., hair and eye color) were made by God; other things (e.g., food, furniture) were invented by humans. Likewise, in the spring of 2012, while riding in our car to a dance lesson, I told Max and Olivia about the "new laws in Alabama" that discriminated against Latinx persons. While asserting that these laws "were not fair," Olivia maintained her faith-taught hold on race saying, "They were just made like that," meaning persons could not help their skin color because it was a God-given characteristic.

From a whiteness perspective, there are problems with this divine account for race, particularly because, according to the beliefs of our church and our family, our biological/genetic characteristics are God-given. Thandeka (1999) wrote that white people cling to genetic definitions of race because it excuses them from thinking of race as socially constructed in ways that enable their hold on power. If race is socially constructed, so are the positive or negative repercussions that come as a result of one's race. Yet, if race is genetically, or in this case divinely, determined, then whites are absolved from playing a role in creating and perpetuating oppressive structures. Thandeka (1999) also explains that, "Whites like to think of themselves as biologically white in order to hide what they'd like to forget: once upon a time they were attacked by whites in their own community because they weren't yet white" (p. 8). Drawing on historical notions of whiteness, Thandeka argues that in the early United States or the U.S. colonies, race was not an organizing hierarchy and persons were oppressed not because of skin color and ethnic identity but because of class differences, meaning that wealthy white men enslaved (both literally and psychologically) other whites. Whites tend to ignore or displace the complexity of how we came to be raced when biological (or divine) messages are illuminated. In fact, with a biological or divine perspective, whites have a reason for not including the study of how we are raced in religious studies, school curricula, or their daily lives.

This notion complicated the already racially-laden messages that infiltrated our lives. Ella, Olivia, and Max received and constructed ideas that were consistent with this denial of race. They were being prevented from—and learned to prevent themselves from—the possibility of race as socially and historically constructed. Yet, this is an important part of dismantling the crippling hold of racism.

*Valuing Difference in Patronizing Ways*

Related to difference, lessons in Sunday School seemed to be developed with the *intent* to communicate that human beings should appreciate difference and honor those different from ourselves. In reality, however, many of those messages were contradictory. One way the children were invited to explore the notion that we should value others was in a Sunday School lesson about Peter and Cornelius, a Jewish man and a Gentile (a non-Jewish man) who became friends during a biblical political period when this was not likely. The teacher's guide provided the following written script to accompany the lesson:

> But God made everybody—and God loves the whole world! Ask Peter and Cornelius who became friends because they realized God loved both of them. Who can you become better friends with even though that person is different from you? (A neighbor, a kid at school, etc.) No matter how different we are from other people, we can still be loving and friendly. We have to remember God loves the whole world, and we should, too.

Even the language of the lesson seems to communicate that *we* (which in the case of my children and our church meant white Christians) are the chosen ones: "No matter how different we are from other people, we can *still* be loving and friendly." The word *still* sends an almost invisible message of superiority and patronization. Likewise the children learned the story of "The Good Samaritan," furthering the notion of difference, albeit also contradictory in its attempt to focus on valuing and caring for those different from oneself. During Sunday School, the teacher pointed out that the Samaritans, according to the Bible, were despised by the Jews and were treated unfairly. The teacher explained that the Jews believed, "The Samaritans don't talk the same [as us], they don't look the same [as us]. We don't want to be nice to them." The story then describes how, in spite of the animosity between Jews and Samaritans, a particular Samaritan cared for a badly beaten Jew left on the side of the road.

Valuing difference was a message contained not in lessons alone but also in texts that filled the church buildings. Bulletin boards stating *"God [loves] the whole world even people who are different from us"* adorned the children's ministry building where all grade level Sunday School classes were held after a lesson on the Bible story of the day. The use of the word *even* in this bulletin board, much like the use of the word *still* in the example above, sends a small subtle message of superiority that was, I believe, linked to race;

thus, while the teachings of our faith are that differences are benign, the reality in which my children live does not send those messages: We do not live near people who are different from us, we do not go to school with many people who are different from us, and we do not worship with people who are different from us. Furthermore, my children learned discourses of difference through discourses of whiteness and Blackness wrapped up in larger messages about pity, exclusion, fear, and so on of, or for, the Other (Miller, 2015).

In addition to patronizing messages inherent in these lessons, the clear irony here is that the children were not in a context, in their hyper-segregated place of worship, where they might have genuinely explored differences with those unlike them although *they were being taught and were learning that loving across differences was a virtue.* In reality, there were few interactions to truly experience people unlike themselves nor were there any opportunities to explore how systemic racism prevents equality in U.S. society. The point to be made here is that the children's experiences in their Christian worlds, while rife with potential to interrupt the construction of whiteness as the norm, as the superior race, in many ways, taught and affirmed those notions.

## LOCATING WHITENESS IN COLONIALISM AND PATRIOTISM

Prolific in this study were recurrent throwbacks to discourses that celebrated English monarchies, confounded with a learned sense of patriotism that contributed to my children's construction of themselves and others as raced. *At the same time* that Ella, Olivia, and Max were washed with prolific monarchical discourses, they were also consumed by a pro-nationalism, pro-westward patriotic discourse.

### Castles Conjure Images of and Celebrate English Monarchies

Although originally built for protection against invaders, castles have long been associated with European power and privilege. Distinct from fortifications used in other cultures around the world, European castles were used for private residential protections for power holders in those societies. In the lives of my children, the castles that decorated their world—in pictures, in books and magazines, in movies and on TV shows, on walls at the doctor's office, in toys, and subsequently through their own recreated images—were the feudal-style castles popular in Europe, adorned with a gatehouse, corner towers, and machicolations. These symbols of power and privilege were incorporated routinely into the children's play. At Olivia's spend-the-night party for her sixth birthday, she and three friends played with a PlayMobile© figurine set, a gift for her birthday. In the play set, the main structure is a castle with small white dolls, horses, drawbridges, and crowns intended to evoke imaginary play. The girls, familiar with the narrative of colonization, immediately put on a play in which racialized violence and adventure were part and parcel of the story line. Olivia, who played the part of a princess, found a sword and gave it to her six-year-old cousin, Summers, who performed the role of a prince. Olivia said, "Here is your sword to fight people." After the girls enacted the meeting and marrying of the prince and princess, the princess "set sail" in a toy table (a pretend ship) carrying her pets to "another land"—Africa. Olivia's friend, Anna Margaret (AM), playing the part of the princess's friend, turned to the princess's new husband (played by Summers) for help in bringing her friend back from her adventure across the ocean:

> Olivia (as the ship sets sail): Get in to go to my Africa. Anyone, hop on the boat. . . . (Overlapping voices as the girls sail to Africa)
> Olivia: I wanna get on the road back home. Where is my kitty, kitty? (The girls sail back home.)
> Olivia (singing): I'm going to ride my horse to Africa, because there is land. I'm going to go, go, go across the ocean. I'm going to go, go across the ocean.

While I do not know why the children chose to reference Africa in this example, it is interesting to note how historically and hauntingly accurate the storyline in their play was—European power holders (i.e., royals) going or sending others to *new* (interpreted-as-new-by-whites), far-away places (Africa) that they claim as their own demonstrated by Olivia singing "get in [the ship] to go to *my* Africa." There were untold parts of the history with which the girls were likely not familiar (the rape of those new lands depicted as adventures but actually constructed with the intent of gaining material wealth at the subjugation and enslavement of dark-skinned Others); however, learning and enacting such a one-sided version of a historical era reinforced notions of white and European dominance.

In this narrative of colonization, the center of the universe was the castle and all of the whiteness it protected inside. As the girls left whiteness, they "sailed" the largest expanse of the physical earth—the ocean—into Blackness represented by Africa. In the girls' fantasy play, the farthest place away from themselves was Africa, etching more deeply into their psyches that the farthest thing from whiteness is Blackness. Fanon's (1967) words come to mind here: "Colonialism is not satisfied merely with holding people in its grip and emptying the native's brain of all form and content. By a kind of perverted logic, it turns to the past of the oppressed people and distorts, disfigures and destroys it" (p. 169). During the fantasy play, the girls both possessed and distanced themselves from Blackness as they sailed from whiteness/the castle to Blackness/Africa, where they claimed Blackness as their own, as Olivia narrated that she was going to "my Africa" because "there is land."

It is not a stretch to speculate where the girls learned the narratives of colonization. These narratives sing through the radio (discussed below), infiltrate media, and are reinforced and recreated time and time again in movies with wide-reaching influence, such as Disney movies. Although Disney is an obvious and frequent source of promotional colonial hegemony (Ott & Mack, 2010), it is not only the Disney stories themselves that recreate history in a way that silences the colonized; it is also the monopolizing power of Disney as a licensing powerhouse that strengthens its strong grip on the narrative of colonization beyond movies, for example, fast food billboards, images on sleeping bags, décor for bedrooms. The recreation of history in this way is an instrument of colonial hegemony because the colonizers' narrative is the only perspective told. The girls were not merely reenacting the script. They were constructing a world where they, in their whiteness, were at the center and Blackness was on the outer fringes, for the taking when they wanted it. While Paley (2004) describes that there is "nothing more dependable and risk-free" as fantasy play and that "dangers are only pretend" (p. 8), I argue that the dangers in colonial fantasy play, easily accessible through symbols like castles, are quite real and quite dangerous: they provide the stage for a reconstruction of white dominance in the white imaginary, further exacerbating the real world of white supremacy.

## Discourses of American Patriotism and Westward Expansion

While the children learned to be raced as the superior white Europeans surrounded with dominant discourses of English monarchies, re-appropriating them into their own lives and play, another competing discourse was apparent. This was a pro-nationalist discourse that celebrated U.S. independence from England, U.S. westward expansion, and U.S. patriotism. For example, Ella and the other members of her school's guitar club learned and performed the popular song "Yankee Doodle " at a school concert. Although originally a satire on early U.S. colonists, the song is generally thought to represent independence from the British.

Likewise, for weeks, Max incessantly sang a song that he learned in music class in school, "You're a Grand Old Flag." Max was so enamored with this patriotic song that he often launched into singing it even when it was not appropriate for him to do so, such as in the middle of a Sunday School lesson. I observed him drawing on his internalization of those words and appropriating them during Sunday School. Interacting with his Sunday School teacher, Ms. Julie, the following exchange occurred:

Ms. Julie: What is something you can do to be a fisherman of Jesus?

Max (sings): I'm a high flying flag! Every heart beats through!

The stories above constitute an addition to the construction of multiple identities in complex ways. Max amalgamated the teachings of Jesus with his
temporally favorite brand of patriotic discourse around the U.S. flag. Both
the Christian discourse and the patriotic discourse are inundated with white
dominance since Jesus was, for my children, decidedly white, and patriotism
was perpetuated as a (white) liberation from England.

In addition to the songs the children learned in school, songs we listened
to on the radio also glamorized a sense of white-based nationalism through a
representation of the *civilizing* of the *Old West* by white settlers. In many
songs, the lyrics expressed a longing to live vicariously through glamorized
U.S. western heroes: tough, protective, adventurous, dangerous, sexy, and
white. Country music singer Toby Keith (1993/1998) wrote and sang the
song, "Should've Been a Cowboy" that romanticizes cowboy life—roping,
riding, wearing six-shooters. Echoes of claiming *new* land for white people
dominant in Wild West narratives of this relatively older song were reflected
in newer music as well and were not necessarily tied to Western U.S. expansion. Well-known singer Brad Paisley celebrates European immigration in a
single entitled "American Saturday Night" (2009) as he narrates how his
ancestors would never have been able to dream, when they stepped off their
immigration ship to America, that their children's children's children would
acquire so much wealth.

In other places and spaces in my children's worlds, the same kind of
narrative continued. For example, to position the young girls to get their
bodies ready for a jazz dance during the pilot study in the fall of 2011, Ella's
dance teacher used language that resurrected images of European conquest
and Western expansion. As she placed her hands to each side of her hips in a
position to draw an imaginary gun from a holster, she said, "OK girls, get
your guns out! Ch-Ch" and she would remind the girls to "Check your guns!
They better be square" frequently throughout the dance lessons. During
stretches, the girls were told to "Pull up to your little teepees," indicating that
they should position their bodies so that they made a triangle with their arms,
legs, and the dance floor. Scolding the girls for incorrect posturing, the dance
teacher said, "Now this shouldn't look like an Indian ceremony, girls." This
language (i.e., white terminology used to describe American Indians and
Wild West lingo) was typical in dance lessons and reflects characteristics of
"white talk" (McIntyre, 1997) in that it served to distance whites from persons of color (in this case, American Indians) by drawing out seemingly
exotic cultural differences (dance ceremonies and religious houses named
teepees), as well as evoking images of fear and needed protection ("get your
guns out"). The assumption, of course, is that the persons in need of protection, or the voyagers naming the exotic, were white people.

The expected implicit (invisible) position through all of this—and the reason that my children's internalization of these blatantly racist/white superiority notions is so important if we are to understand how they constructed notions about whiteness—is that over and over, white narrators told stories of white adventure and triumph. As they did this, they simultaneously sent messages of negativity, fear, and diminished skill and intelligence regarding people of color. Although race is rarely mentioned explicitly (except in the case of the dance teacher), the implication of white superiority in each instance is glaringly obvious.

## CONCLUSION

In this chapter, I argued that the dominant discourses that shaped three young white children's construction of race, particularly what it means to be white, did not operate in isolation from one another. They overlapped in murky yet very powerful and influential ways. I found through analysis of my data that it was impossible to study race alone when everything my children were coming to understand about race was also mediated by class, religious, colonial, and patriotic discourses. Because multiple, overlapping systems of oppression exist, attempting to make sense of how they overlap is important. In fact, the very fact that they *do* overlap in such insidious ways gives systems of oppression much of their power. Each system of power gives energy to other systems of power: for my family, Christianity fueled classism and racism, but racism and classism also defined the Christian perspectives we believed and all of this was grounded from a deliberately and insidiously taught pro-nationalist discourse. Beginning to sift through this complexity to center race and racism, without ignoring how other systems of oppression work in conjunction with racism, is a necessary part of understanding white children's construction of race.

And, from understanding, action beckons. As a white mother, I learned to do things to counter the insidious racism in our lives (for more on practical strategies that came out of this study, see Miller, 2015): I taught explicit lessons on the value and contributions of African epistemologies; we engaged in conversations about the ways that only seeing pictures of a white Jesus contributes to Christian racism; we looked together—as a family—for Advent calendars that did not showcase a white Santa (and, despite extensive searches, we never could find any, which was a powerful lesson in and of itself). We talked openly about race and racism and the way neighborhoods (including our own) were formed on racist ideology. Once, years after the study, when reflecting on how often I brought up race and racism compared to other white adults he knew, Max said, "Mama, you are a very unusual white woman." This seemed to capture the essence of our trouble as white people: until talking about and responding to race and racism is no longer unusual among white families, these stealthy messages of whiteness will maintain their gripping hold on white identity formation.

## REFERENCES

Aboud, F. E. (2003). The formation of in-group favoritism and out-group prejudice in young children: Are they distinct attitudes? *Developmental Psychology, 39*(1), 48-60.

Bissex, G. (1980). *Gnyx at work: A child learns to read and write.* Cambridge, MA: Harvard University Press.

Brown, R. (2010). *Prejudice: Its social psychology* (2nd Ed.). Cambridge, MA: John Wiley & Sons.

Butler, D. (1980). *Babies need books: How to share the joy of reading with your child.* New York: Atheneum.

Collins, S. (2008). *The hunger games.* New York: Scholastic.

Deliovsky, K. (2010). *White femininity: Race, gender & power.* Halifax and Winnipeg: Fernwood Publishing.

Fanon, F. (1967). *The wretched of the earth.* New York: Grove Press.

Foucault, M. (1972). *The archaeology of knowledge and the discourse on language.* New York: Pantheon Books.

Freund, D. M. P. (2007). *Colored property: State policy and white racial politics in suburban America.* Chicago, IL: University of Chicago Press.

Keith, T. (1998). *Should've been a cowboy.* Greatest Hits [CD]. Nashville, TN: Mercury.

Lareau, A., & Conley, D. (Eds.). (2008). *Social class: How does it work?* New York: Russell Sage Foundation.

Long, S. (2004). Passionless text and phonics first: Through a child's eyes. *Language Arts, 81*(5), 417-426.

Martens, P. (1996). *I already know how to read: A child's view of literacy.* Portsmouth, NH: Heinemann.

McIntyre, A. (1997). *Making meaning of whiteness: Exploring racial identity with white teachers.* Albany, NY: State University of New York Press.

McNamee, S. J., & Miller, R. K. (2009). *The meritocracy myth.* Lanham, MD: Rowman & Littlefield Publishers.

Miller, E. T. (2015). Discourses of whiteness and blackness: An ethnographic study of three young children learning to be white. *Ethnography and Education, 10*(2), 137-153.

Miller, E. T. (2016). Multiple pathways to whiteness: White teachers' unsteady racial identities. *Early Years, 37*(1), 17-33.

Miller, E. T. (2017). The murky and mediated experiences of white identities in early childhood. In S. Hancock & C. A. Warren (Eds.), *White women's work: Examining the intersectionality of teaching, identity, and race* (pp. 123-146). Scottsdale, AZ: Information Age Publishing.

Moon, D. (1999). White enculturation and bourgeois ideology. In T. K. Nakayama & J. N. Martin (Eds.), *Whiteness: The communication of social identity* (pp. 177-197). Thousand Oaks, CA: SAGE Publications.

Morris, J. E., & Monroe, C. R. (2009). Why study the US South?: The nexus of race and place in investigating Black student achievement. *Educational Researcher, 38*(1), 21-36.

Ott, B. L., & Mack, R. L. (2010). *Critical media studies: An introduction.* Malden, MA. John Wiley & Sons.

Paisley, B. (2009). *Another Saturday Night* (CD). Franklin, TN: Arista Nashville.

Paley, V. G. (2004). *A child's work: The importance of fantasy play.* Chicago, IL: University of Chicago Press.

Redmond, M. (2005). *Blessed be Your Name.* (CD). Survivor Records.

Sullivan, S. (2004). White world traveling. *The Journal of Speculative Philosophy,* 18(4), 300-304.

Thandeka (1999). *The cost of whiteness*. Retrieved from: http://infidelity.blogsome.com

Tyson, T. B. (2005). *Blood done sign my name: A true story*. New York: Broadway Books.

Van Avermaet, E., & McClintock, C. G. (1988). Intergroup fairness and bias in children. *European Journal of Social Psychology, 18*(5), 407-427.

*Chapter Two*

# Walking the Walk, or Walking on Eggshells: Silence and the Limits of White Privilege

## Christina Berchini

I remember visiting my parents' friends as a child. Their friends—a white couple with their young, white daughter in tow—traveled from their home in the south (I could tell by their accents) to visit extended family who lived in Brooklyn, New York. They were staying just a few short miles from where I lived with my family.

When we arrived, I sat with my parents in an unfamiliar kitchen, a bit bored while they caught up with their friends. As is often the case when catching-up involves children, the conversation turned to schooling (e.g., How is school going? Do you like it? What's your favorite subject?). Their daughter, a fair-skinned blonde somewhere around my age (ten or eleven years old at the time) proudly—even *dutifully*—announced that she did not talk to the Black boys in her class. Her father complimented her obedience, and reminded her, in front of me, in front of my family, of their "rule": "That's right, you do not talk to *those* kids." My parents remained silent; my mom looked a bit uncomfortable. A profound sense of confusion usurped my boredom.

I questioned my parents during the short car ride home to our apartment. They glanced at each other and voiced disapproval toward their friends for being "a little bit racist" and reminded me that no, in fact *no*, I had not been raised that way. I relaxed, both physically and emotionally, confident in my interpretation of the unfortunate dialogue that unfolded in that kitchen. That family was wrong; my family was right. We were not racist, and as a child, that was all I needed to know. After all, I went to school in Brooklyn, New York, with a lot of children of color, and conversing with them was normal.

My elementary school was incredibly diverse, and I had friends of all kinds—I was neither encouraged to, nor prohibited from, having a racially, ethnically, linguistically, or socioeconomically diverse group of friends. I didn't think about the incident again, until much further down the line.

This childhood memory provides the backdrop for what has become something of a strange and confusing path toward the antiracist work to which I am committed. My trajectory to becoming white is a windy one, with significant twists, turns, dilemmas, and losses. My childhood memory might make it seem that I was poised to navigate whiteness and pursue antiracist work in ways that would have been met, at the very least, with the quiet support of my family. Rather, my pursuits have left my closest relationships strained, and at times, devastated—an impact on my personal life that left me unprepared for the consequences of becoming a "race traitor" (Trainor, 2002, p. 633) in my quest to "disown [my] unearned privileges and fight to reform the institutions that conferred such privileges on [me]" (Haviland, 2008, p. 44). Moreover, my pursuits have also forced me to consider the consequences of my own critical pedagogies (Trainor, 2002; see also Berchini, 2017). In short, extant research on whiteness and antiracism has called out educators and scholars for not recognizing or dealing with or dismantling racialized privilege (see Haviland, 2008; Picower, 2009), but if my experiences are any indication, there are real consequences for doing this kind of work—like the dissolution or loss of once-close relationships.

With this chapter I contribute to a nascent yet growing corpus of work that addresses the emotions associated with ambivalent white identities (Chubbuck & Zembylas, 2008; A. Lensmire, 2012; T. Lensmire, 2010): fear, loss, anxiety, and commitment, all wrapped up to form one confused, racial state of being. Following Thandeka's (1999) argument that one "learns [to be white] as a self-protection against racial abuse from its own community" (p. 137), Audrey Lensmire (2012) describes white teachers as emerging from inherently ambivalent selves as a function of "acts of violence by white authority against its own white community" (p. 160). Violence, in my case, is symbolic: The success of my adult relationship with my mother, and several other family members, is predicated on my silence about whiteness, racism, and social justice, lest I wish to decimate my closest relationships. The requirement that I remain silent is never imposed upon me explicitly; rather, it is implied. It dangles above me, a threatening reminder that I have much to lose if I do not comply with its demands.

## WALKING THE WALK

All things considered there is no positive spin on "race" and racism because "race" is a construct that is used to differentiate, (dis)advantage, and (dis)empower each time it is uncritically invoked. Even positive social transformation will involve remarking upon these racialised concepts and processes and to this end, simply, involves telling someone something about themselves/ the world that needs to change. (Hylton, 2012, p. 36)

I wish to make clear: As a teacher, researcher, and lifelong student, I am committed to the ongoing fight against racism in society and institutions. I do not disagree with the ways in which scholars have theorized whiteness in relation to racism. I do not argue with the idea that whiteness depends on racism in order to achieve/perpetuate/maintain its dominance in society. I do not argue with the idea that whiteness should be recognized, examined, and interrogated, as it plays out in institutions of education. I do not argue against the reality that I, a white woman, have benefited, in real, tangible, and symbolic ways, from racist structures and institutions designed and determined to oppress my peers of color.

I used to believe that, in matters of fighting racism, I was committed to not only talking the talk, but walking the walk. Hylton (2012) defines walking the walk as "agitat[ing] for change and . . . [a willingness] to defend positions that are marginal, challenging, and sometimes plain unpopular" (p. 36). Hylton's take resonates with Haviland's (2008), who argues that

one of the outcomes of silence in discussions of race, racism, and White supremacy can be a lack of challenges to dominant perspectives. This lack of challenges, in turn, can reinforce the status quo that Whites enforce and from which they benefit. (p. 47)

Taken together, it would seem that there is not room for silence in the struggle to walk the walk toward white antiracist work; to remain silent during teachable moments is to talk a good game in theory, but to fail in the execution of goals for antiracist action.

There are, however, problems with this metaphor: Firstly, it holds that there is a "right" way of pursuing antiracist work (however elusive), and/or that silence is, unambiguously, a bad thing. Extant scholarship has come under fire for ignoring the emotional violence that is committed against whites for attempting—and failing at—walking the walk (see Lensmire et al., 2013). While "talking the talk" *and* "walking the walk" are metaphors that have given articulation to the work of antiracism in professional and scholarly spaces, my attempts to "walk the walk" in personal spaces (e.g., my working-class home community) have ultimately rendered me—quite literally—without words *or* action.

# WALKING ON EGGSHELLS

Walking on eggshells appears to be a more apt metaphor for conducting antiracist work in my personal life. In other words, what happens when antiracist goals are thwarted as a whiteness scholar and educator attempts to "walk the walk" in their home community, say, during a telephone call, or at the dinner table with friends and family? When the recognition, examination, and interrogation of white privilege and white supremacy throw important relationships into a state of perpetual upheaval? When commitments to "walking the walk" and fighting against white supremacist and racist per- spectives cause rifts and long periods of silence with the people who matter most, particularly family members who may have served as your earliest teachers? When your life's work has resulted in emotional pain and loss, injurious to relationships at one time considered strong, secure, predictable, and perhaps unbreakable?

In this discussion, I follow up on the vignette with which I began this chapter, by sharing two stories featuring troubling interactions—specifically those that occurred with my mother. I've chosen to feature this relationship because it represents one of the bumpier, more confusing, and ultimately disheartening impasses toward antiracist work that I have faced. Indeed, the woman who made sure to raise my sister and me to know that racism is wrong is the same woman whom I now struggle, as an adult, to understand— particularly in conversations when she freely (and fiercely) associates crime, drugs, and unfit parenting with people of color, and terrorism with Muslim populations, and always as if there is no other, perhaps more nuanced expla- nation for any social issue. Most dishearteningly, my mother knows of the kind of work that I do—it seems that our struggles began when my work began, and in ways that have often felt antagonistic.

I also feature glimpses into this relationship because it forces me to won- der what my students are up against as a result of my own teaching: That is, what do my students—all of whom are novice teachers—face when they set out to work toward antiracist and transformative ends? The sort of transfor- mative work that, in some ways, I hope I've taught them to take on (see Berchini, 2017)? What are the (un)spoken stories that have made this work so difficult? In what ways do they receive support (or not) for whatever antiracist action they hope to take in their schools and lives? I chose the vignettes that follow to shed insights into the limitations of theorizing white- ness strictly according to a discourse and analysis of white privilege (see Berchini, 2017; Lensmire et al., 2013). I chose these stories, also, to shed insights into the limitations I confront, as a professional and also a person. In matters of antiracism, the two are forever conjoined.

## Vignette #1: What is My Daughter Going to Say about White People this Time?

As I mention in the childhood memory with which I begin this chapter, I was neither encouraged to, nor prohibited from, interacting with children who were not white, or who differed from my own racial and cultural background in some way. Years later when, as a teenager, I took a romantic interest in a mixed-race boy whom I met when visiting my grandparents in Florida, the response was similar. My parents did not take issue with my love interest, and even denounced my grandparents' horrifically racist attitude toward my adolescent relationship: "Stick to your own kind," my grandparents would admonish, and often.

It was not until I became active in my personal and professional commitments toward antiracism that the pain and anxiety really began. By the time of this vignette, I was near the completion of my PhD in curriculum, instruction, and teacher education. My work centered on investigating white teachers' racial identity development. The terms white privilege, white supremacy, and institutionalized racism became regular, even daily components of my vocabulary—both at work and home.

It wasn't long before I began to notice that my professional and personal commitments to antiracism seemed to coincide with the worst of the screaming matches. One parental visit in particular taught me a great deal about silence when my mother left my apartment and Michigan in tears, shielded from me by my stepfather's strong, supportive embrace, after a heated discussion in my living room. In this discussion, she detailed the myriad ways by which she experienced "reverse racism" during her time as a postal employee. An explanation of institutionalized racism from her daughter was not well-received; her experiences were "proof positive" of "reverse racism," and something about which I, her "child," was not qualified to argue, as I had "never experienced life in the post office," education be damned. These claims were particularly confusing when I remembered how, not ten years prior, we spent several holidays at our home with people of color—my mother's friends from her job at the post office.

Several months of tense silence followed this event.

In other, less heated conversations about race, racism, and whiteness, my mother expressed a sincere hope that my research would not "hurt" me when it came time to find a job the following year, that it would not diminish my chances of making a living, post-graduate studies. As a graduate student with enough to worry about at the time, her concerns only (however irrationally) fueled my own:

*What if she's right?* For one full evening, I sat on my couch, head in hands, fully convinced that I would not land a job thanks to my work with whiteness and antiracism. These types of interactions with my mother and others, however explosive or mild, have conditioned my silence toward matters of race when it comes to my personal relationships.

As I describe below, it would seem that—despite my intentions—I have become the "critical educator" who has chosen to neither talk the talk *nor* walk the walk during moments teachable. I have become the very caricature about whom critical race scholarship warns. For Hylton (2012), "Researching racialised problematics ultimately leads scholars to a point where they *must agitate for change and unfortunately be willing to defend positions that are marginal, challenging, and sometimes plain unpopular*" (p. 36, italics added). Here again, silence in matters of race and racism is not an option. However, it was not until I began reading literature on ambivalent white identities and critiques of critical pedagogies that I began to theorize the reasons for my silence. One visit with my mother and stepfather stands out in particular.

"Help me understand, what is your research about again?"

My stepfather asked me this question during a biennial (and perhaps, from his perspective, obligatory) trip to Lansing, Michigan, with my mother. We've had a rocky five years, since I callously left my home and family on the east coast to pursue graduate studies in the Midwest. This is a foreign endeavor to a family consisting predominantly of civil servants (i.e., mass transit and postal workers). Education—up until my generation—was something to be completed through high school. My mother, pregnant with me at her high school graduation, did not have the option of attending college. My father jokes about how his community college invited him to disenroll after his short stint of (unsuccessfully) attempting to take classes while supporting his new family. My stepfather, designated "Man of the House" at the age of four when his own father passed away, could not justify furthering his education when he had a mother and younger brothers to support, financially and emotionally. In all of this, I realized a long time ago that not everyone is likely to appreciate my goals; that is, being related does not guarantee the emotional support one might expect when she is about to embark on a long road to . . . who knows where.

Given several years' worth of tension, I've learned to clam up when my mother and stepfather ask me about my work, and particularly when my work, a few short semesters after I began my graduate studies, took a turn for the critical.

"Well. . ." I hesitated. This wasn't the first time a family member asked me about my work. Admittedly, I've come to fear such questions, as the conversations which result tend to end bitingly, heatedly, often abruptly, and sometimes tearfully, when we, usually red-faced and breathless, hastily shut each other up by agreeing to disagree. I continued on quickly, and just about at the level of a mutter. In an attempt to keep it simple, I responded: "I'm studying how white teachers navigate issues related to race in their teaching, curriculum, classrooms, schools, and lives."

I braced myself. My stepfather asked a few questions about what I meant; I have (un/intentionally) blocked most of his questions from memory, but remember one in particular: "Wait, isn't a teacher's job to just teach the subject?" I am, though, typically forgiving of this question, as many people outside—and even inside of—education do not much consider the racial and power politics embedded in subject matter and curriculum, or, as Yosso (2010) states, the "racism, sexism, classism, and other forms of subordination in formal and hidden curricular structures, processes, and discourses" (p. 99). My mother remained characteristically quiet; she has, I think, learned to fear these conversations as much as I have. She—we both—tap dance around conversations about race and whiteness, likely for fear that our next argument or blowout will be our last (and indeed sometimes it feels this way). But this time, her facial expression was unmistakably skeptical, perhaps even concerned. Because I know her—because I know *us*—I knew damned well what she was thinking: "Jesus *Christ*, what is my daughter going to say about white people *this time*, and how is that going to make *me* look?"

I have learned to dread these conversations with my parents, and do anything possible to change the subject. My family, as with many white people, often relates these kinds of conversations to "the personal" in an attempt to explain away and perhaps even justify any number of harmful ideas about race and racism, without any critical understanding of how racism is reinforced institutionally. In other words, they lack critical knowledge of how, "even as individual racial prejudices declines, structural racist patterns persist and are attributable to the inertia of U.S. institutional cultures and practices" (Gusa, 2010, p. 465). I understand this. As my stepfather is wont to remind me, "not everyone is a graduate student." To be sure, he is correct. Not everyone has read Noguera, hooks, Delpit, Carter Andrews, Sleeter, Wise, or any of the myriad scholars who have so thoughtfully and brilliantly contributed to—and extended—the discussion about institutionalized racism, whiteness, and white supremacy, namely in relationship to education. But I have. I have engaged this scholarship deeply, have made it my life's work, and—in the process—am learning to turn a critical eye to my own existence as a (relatively) privileged white female.

While this moment with my parents appeared to be a teachable one, it was not one I was in any rush to take advantage of. In this case, and once again, silence prevailed. This moment represents what our discussions about my work have eventually become—we avoid any sort of deep conversations with each other about matters of race.

Thankfully, we reached our destination at that point in the conversation, and I was able to drown my anxieties in an overpriced, whipped-cream-topped espresso drink. I have not been able to find a way to describe my sense of relief as I relish in those "bullet-dodged" kinds of moments. For Audrey Lensmire (2012), "Not speaking or remaining silent about race is commonplace. . . . White people are not supposed to talk about race, nor does it matter either way" (p. 18). To be sure, my deflections and avoidances are a privilege of whiteness; it might seem that I can forego a deeper, more complex conversation about my work without suffering any real consequences. On the other hand, my silence about matters of race, in relation to my work, is not a privilege; it does not feel like one, and it does not get enacted as one. My relationship with my mother and other family members relies on artful deflections, avoidance, and remaining silent about the issues I hold dear. To reduce my silence to a "privilege" feels under-theorized and incomplete. Yes—at a surface level, it is a "privilege" to remain silent about race. But it feels more like pain, frustration, and the constant need to avoid walking the walk in favor of walking the line barefooted, a line littered with jagged eggshells.

### Vignette #2: "I'm Sorry, but I Associate Mosques with Terrorism."

About two years after the first vignette took place (and six months after—thankfully—beginning my new professorship), I began blogging. Blogging is my way to continue writing during those inevitable days when intellectual heavy-lifting (by way of writing) is not an option, due to time constraints or something else. Furthermore, blogging about my work has provided opportunities to frame conversations I care about in ways that are accessible and interesting to wider audiences, and is a personal goal of mine.

One such day, I decided to blog about a conversation I had with my mother the evening before. An excerpt from the blog post is as follows:

"We got dressed to go to the gym, but decided to put our house on the market instead," my mother casually delivered this news to me on the phone and across the 1100 miles that now separate us. She was in the middle of preparing dinner; I was in the middle of a powerwalk.

"Uh….what?" Her news threw me. She and my stepfather bought their home eight years ago. It was their first home. Have they even broken it in yet?

"What happened?" I was genuinely curious about how one leaps from going to the gym to listing their home on the market. But, I have not yet learned that simple questions like "what happened?" are dangerous questions. And not only are they dangerous questions, but they are also painful reminders of how my relationship with my mother has changed over the last six years.

"The neighbors' backyard smells like dog shit and it's wafting over into our yard and I am sick of it. And there's another Mosque going up and I'm sorry, but I associate Mosques with terrorism."

Interesting, I thought. My view of churches might be chalked up similarly. I no longer say these things aloud, though. My relationship with my mother depends on it.

I have several reasons for sharing this excerpt; first, the experience represents profound confusion, particularly when juxtaposed with the memory with which I began this chapter. I was not raised to maintain ignorant or hateful views; the views that my mother freely expresses now are not views to which I was exposed while growing up, at least not consciously, explicitly, or openly. The devolution of my relationship with my mother has made for terrifically complicated engagements with (my) whiteness, the ways by which I enact and legitimate whiteness (Castagno, 2008), and the ways by which whiteness and white supremacy have, for me personally, damaged my relationship with the most important woman in my life.

Secondly, the post achieved significant attention upon being featured on a popular blogging website. Reactions were immediate and plentiful; some were supportive; many others served as reminders of the silencing power of whiteness (Haviland, 2008). Within minutes, I was labeled "selfish" and "despicable" (by white women), and informed that I "should be ashamed" of myself; I suspected that my mother, if she were to see the post, would agree with such reactions. Even though I posted anonymously, I became concerned—however irrationally—that the post would somehow find its way to her inbox and that she'd identify me as the author. I asked website moderators to remove the post, a request they surprisingly honored. Once again, silence prevailed (Castagno, 2008); I silenced and reversed my own efforts to take part in a public discussion within which I attempted to grapple with the pain and confusion embedded in struggling with a troubling discourse that, once again, played out surprisingly close to home.

## SILENCE AND THE LIMITS OF WHITE PRIVILEGE

As Audrey Lensmire (2012) observes, "white racial identities are multifarious messes of thought and feeling, and . . . resistance to antiracist and social justice efforts is not always a straightforward defense of white privilege" (p. 170). The vignettes I share above have several purposes. For one, and of necessity, they represent only a sampling of instances during which I struggle with what it means to talk the talk *and* walk the walk; as I argue earlier, in the struggle to support and carry out white antiracist work, the professional and personal, are entwined. There is no leaving the work at the office, only to pick it up again the next morning. That being said, my goal was to offer a nuanced take of some of the ways by which I have been positioned within my white community (despite my work), as an adult who is able to recall a childhood in which racism was not outwardly supported or condoned as a belief system.[1] As an adult who has chosen antiracism as her life's work, silence has taken an unfortunate shape: A combination of silence and avoidance has served the important function of maintaining ties (however tenuous, at times) with my family, and namely, the only mother I will ever have.

Furthermore, a period of silence typically followed the more explosive arguments. Silence has been wielded against me as punishment for what I imagine was internalized by my mother and others as a form of racial (and familial) treason. On one hand, Trainor (2002) explains how the "race traitor" is considered by some to be the only "legitimate white stance" (p. 633) in matters of pursuing and supporting white antiracism and social justice; on the other hand, my stance toward issues of race, racism, and whiteness has had deleterious effects on my relationships, effects that are certainly not to my benefit. While such breaks, at times, were needed, they were not a privilege; they were a consequence. One painful, extended, and *necessary* period of silence occurred during my dissertation and job-seeking year when, in truth, I would have preferred—and benefited from—the love and support of my family.

## WHAT TO DO?

In all of this, I am not an innocent victim. While I have chosen "silence" in these scenarios, I have also been taught a great deal about the discourse of white privilege, and the ways by which it does not hold a lot of stock with those who cannot relate, or those who do not see the value of a counterargument that goes beyond what their own personal experiences have been, particularly in relationship to larger, institutional constructs. As I illustrate above, the ways by which my identity as a contributor to white antiracism intersects and conflicts with my family, I am quite sure, has induced feelings of familial disloyalty, and perhaps even racial treason. Trainor (2002) offers an interesting discussion of the confusions critical white people experience over "how to represent those who are positioned, because of the spaces they occupy in a hierarchically ordered social terrain, as the antagonists in the quest for social justice" (p. 633). In her work with teacher education students, Trainor argues for a need to think differently about those whom we are educating for antiracist and social justice work: "We struggle to represent whiteness and white students as perpetrators of injustice who must be taught to disavow whiteness, and as legitimate social actors on whom we must risk 'an act of love'" (p. 634). While Trainor's work pertains to the educational context, it also speaks to a broader need for a language of anti-essentialism, a language I need to learn for when I return home, as I know that I, too, am complicit in my mother's deep frustrations and our ensuing anxieties in relationship to these (often dreaded) conversations.

## Silence and Interpretation as an Act of Love

I would be remiss if I suggested that there is a "cure" or solution with which to address the contradictions, pain, and frustrations those who support white antiracist work might face in daily life. However, I would also be remiss if I did not feel the need to re/consider my approach to these conversations. A growing body of literature acknowledges the need for a nuanced treatment of whiteness, specifically in relationship to educational contexts (Berchini, 2014, 2017; Flynn, Lensmire, & Lewis, 2009; T. Lensmire, 2010; Trainor, 2002). Timothy Lensmire (2010), for example, observes that "[c]ritical educators have begun to worry that the very way that we have imagined and conceptualized White people and their racial identities is contributing to our critical education failures with them" (p. 169). In a section titled "From liberation to love," Trainor (2002) discusses the limitations of a critical pedagogy in relationship to whiteness, and offers a warning:

> We need to be more aware of the rhetorical frames our pedagogies provide for students as they structure identity. We need to examine the ways that critical pedagogy fails to problematize adequately the different means by which race influences and shapes the dynamic and the results of critical teaching. Without such examination, we risk promoting a devastatingly unintended consequence: the development of a conscious essentialized, and angry white identity predicated on reactionary political values. (p. 647)

While these sentiments are intended to apply to critical pedagogy in the teacher education context, I believe they have broad applicability to those spaces in between and outside of the classroom, those spaces in which conscious and critical white people find themselves struggling with and against their white counterparts who appear to actively defend their positions of privilege. I am inspired by Trainor's (2002) work, and ask: Might silence be reimagined—reinterpreted—as something more than complicity with the status quo?

It is time, I think, for a reinterpretation of silence and love.

Freire (1970) suggests risking an act of love when faced with frameworks, perspectives, and stories that might, at first, leave us feeling extreme discomfort. For Freire,

> Dialogue cannot exist . . . in the absence of a profound love for the world and for people. The naming of the world, which is an act of creation and re-

creation, is not possible if it is not infused with love. Love is at the same time the foundation of dialogue and dialogue itself. . . . Because love is an act of courage, not of fear, love is commitment to others. . . . If I do not love the world—if I do not love life—if I do not love people—I cannot enter into dialogue. (pp. 89-90)

I find it appropriate to circle back to Freire's prescient and moving words as a way to advance this discussion. Freire was not only motivated by hope; he was motivated by love. To this end, I am reminded of a whiteness scholar highly influential to my own work. Audrey Lensmire (2012) reminds readers that "Stories are important" (p. 67). As poignantly, she notes that "listening is important" (p. 67). Listening to each other's stories, and honoring each other's experiences—and *especially* those perspectives that challenge our own—is important. Moreover, it is an act of love (see Tanner & Berchini, 2017, for an extended discussion).

I also remain inspired by Thandeka's (1999) powerful work, and am reminded of my own experiences when she argues that stories about white racial identity formation are not strictly

stories about white racism, privilege, or race pride. They are stories about children and adults who learned how to think of themselves as white in order to stay out of trouble with their caretakers and in the good graces of their peers of the enforcers of community racial standards. . . . they simply [want] to remain within their own community—or at least not to be abandoned by it (p. 20).

Silence, then, as envisioned by Thandeka, acts on those who desire (or require) the support of their family and communities. Granted, I am no longer a child with a desire—a *need*—to "stay out of trouble." My emotional and economic livelihood no longer rely on neutral (or even positive) relationships with my parents and family. However, the narratives I offer here signal that the conflict of choosing between antiracism and maintaining loving familial relationships can and does extend far beyond childhood. Silence is not a choice I've made in a vacuum. That I am rendered complicit in maintaining the status quo—however this might be defined in a given moment—is certainly a seductive interpretation of my white racial identity development. But it is also insufficient.

In the spirit of interpreting silence as (possibly) a loving act, I conclude with this: My mother is a complex woman. If studying whiteness has taught me anything over time, it's that she is more than a discriminatory comment about a mosque. And really, what should I (we) expect her to say, when she—along with many other white people—is receiving damaging and violent media messages about non-whites, non-Christians, people who are poor, and other groups at every possible turn? Moreover, "white privilege" is the sort of academic discourse (Berchini, 2017) that would have allowed for a more critical stance regarding the myth of "reverse racism" about which my mother and I went head-to-head. As a working-class woman, she did not have access to this discourse. With roots and a family deeply entrenched in the working-class, it would be more than twenty-five years before I would access the discourse of "white privilege" through masters' and doctoral work. What chance, really, do people have to deconstruct their own learning about race, whiteness, and racism without intentionally seeking it out (e.g., through graduate study, as I had)? Moreover, discourses of racism and Islamophobia are bigger than her; they are bigger than our relationship. This reality makes imagery of "walking the walk" unambiguously idealistic, tenuous, and, in many ways, unrealistic.

Finally, Trainor (2002) argues that, "we may . . . have to find ways, paradoxically, to embrace discourses" (p. 647) that might seem, at the surface, unembraceable:

> In the end, if we are to deconstruct, even abolish, whiteness as a political and ideological construct, if we are to be "race traitors" as well as teachers, we may first have to find ways, paradoxically, to embrace discourses that we might have once "preferred not to honor, even with our gaze." (pp. 647-648)

My parents are not my students, but my mother's tears might suggest a need for me to be more cognizant of the "rhetorical frames" I employ when I engage family members with discussions about my work. Just as I wish for my own stories (as with those I share above) to be honored and embraced, my mother is likely seeking the same (as with her experiences in the workplace). My mother has her own stories, stories that are no less real or valid than my own. She too walks the line and errs on the side of silence; I suspect that, like me and albeit for different reasons, she believes our relationship depends on it. For both us, a white supremacist society has provided the jagged eggshells on which we walk when we are with each other. Silence and love have worked in tandem to act on the both of us. In dealing with whiteness, family, and home communities, there is only walking on eggshells.

## REFERENCES

Berchini, C. (2014). *Teachers constructing and being constructed by prevailing discourses and practices of whiteness in their curriculum, classroom, and school community: A critical inquiry of three first-year English teachers* (Unpublished doctoral dissertation). Retrieved from Proquest, LLC, database. (UMI No. 3630576).

Berchini, C. (2017). Critiquing un/critical pedagogies to move toward a pedagogy of responsibility in teacher education. *Journal of Teacher Education, 68*(5), 463-475. doi: 10.1177/0022487117702572

Castagno, A. E. (2008). "I don't want to hear that!": Legitimating whiteness through silence in schools. *Anthropology & Education Quarterly, 39*(3), 314-333.

Chubbuck, S. M., & Zembylas, M. (2008). The emotional ambivalence of socially just teaching: A case study of a novice urban schoolteacher. *American Educational Research Journal*, *45*(2), 274-318.

Flynn, J., Lensmire, T., & Lewis, C. (2009). A critical pedagogy of race in teacher education: Response and responsibility. In S. L. Groenke & J. A. Hatch (Eds.), *Critical pedagogy and teacher education in the neoliberal era: Small openings* (pp. 85-98) . New York: Springer.

Freire, P. (1970). *Pedagogy of the oppressed.* New York: Continuum.

Gusa, D. L. (2010). White institutional presence: The impact of Whiteness on campus climate. *Harvard Educational Review, 80*(4), 464-489.

Haviland, V. S. (2008). "Things get glossed over": Rearticulating the silencing power of Whiteness in education. *Journal of Teacher Education, 59*(1), 40-54.

Hylton, K. (2012). Talk the talk, walk the walk: Defining Critical Race Theory in research. *Race Ethnicity and Education, 15*(1), 23-41.

Lensmire, A. (2012). *White urban teachers: Stories of fear, violence, and desire.* Lanham, MD: Rowman & Littlefield Education.

Lensmire, T. J., McManimon, S. K., Tierney, J. D., Lee-Nichols, M. E., Casey, Z. A., Lensmire, A., & Davis, B. M. (2013). McIntosh as synecdoche: How teacher education's focus on white privilege undermines antiracism. *Harvard Educational Review, 83*(3), 410-431.

Lensmire, T. (2010). Ambivalent white racial identities: Fear and an elusive innocence. *Race, Ethnicity and Education,* 13(2), 159-172.

Picower, B. (2009). The unexamined whiteness of teaching: How white teachers maintain and enact dominant racial ideologies. *Race, Ethnicity and Education, 12*(2), 197-215.

Scheurich, J. J. (1993). Toward a white discourse on white racism. *Educational Researcher, 22*(8), 5-10.

Thandeka. (1999). *Learning to be white: Money, race, and God in America.* New York: Continuum.

Tanner, S., & Berchini, C. (2017). Seeking rhythm in white noise: The difficulties embedded in work with whiteness. *English Teaching: Practice and Critique, 16*(1), 40-54.

Trainor, J. S. (2002). Critical pedagogy's "other": Constructions of Whiteness in education for social change. *CCC, 53*(4), 631-650.

Yosso, T. J. (2010). Toward a critical race curriculum. *Equity and Excellence, 35*(2), 93-107.

# NOTES

1. Lest I be misunderstood, I am well aware that not being raised racist does not offer much relief from the realities of institutionalized racism and the fact that I "enjoy" myriad privileges and benefits as a white woman. For Scheurich (1993), "all Whites are socially positioned as Whites and receive social advantages because of this positionality. No individual White gets to be an exception because of his or her antiracism" (p. 9). Regardless of what my parents condoned and believed, I am not an exception because of my antiracism. The point to discussing the kind of environment in which I was raised is to provide a backdrop for the confusion I feel, as an adult, when I find myself in difficult, frustrating, and sometimes even odd conversations with my mother, a woman who never expressed hateful views about diversity when I was a child.

# Chapter Three

# Whiteness as Chaos and Weakness: Our "Abnormal" White Lives

## Samuel Jaye Tanner and Audrey Lensmire

We must be the doctor. –Victoria

We write at the edge. We write as if our lives depend on it. –Jeff Park, *Writing at the Edge*

When Sam joined the Midwest Critical Whiteness Collective he brought an unmatched exuberance. His storytelling about a year-long ethnographic study of his mostly white high school students' critical inquiry into whiteness and their subsequent playbuilding often came back to one particular student he called Victoria. Victoria confided in Sam. She talked about her history with and experiences of depression and also shared her outside-of-school writing about whiteness and the inquiry project with him.

Sam's animated storytelling, questioning, and theorizing about his research and teaching included fragments of his personal narrative. He would run his hands through his short hair, sigh, and mention his messed-up parents and his messed-up childhood. Audrey noticed these references and took them seriously. She became curious to know more about Sam's stories. The personal was central to her work describing and theorizing white teachers and mental health and well-being (Lensmire, 2012; Lensmire & Schick, 2017).

The opportunity for us (Sam and Audrey) to learn more about each other's "messed-up" parents and childhoods arose when Sam brought Victoria's "Venn Diagram of Fun" (see description below) to talk about at a monthly MCWC meeting. Our purpose here is not to trace Sam's teaching project that inspired Victoria's diagram (see Tanner, 2016; Tanner, 2017a; Tanner, 2017b), nor will we share the large corpus of her writing. Instead, we explore how Victoria's Venn diagram, a sophisticated comparing and contrasting of whiteness and depression, provided an opportunity for us to better understand our childhoods.

According to Victoria, whiteness and depression share these *things* (for lack of a better word) or are alike because they

1. are both powerful
2. are not things we chose and are not things we can get rid of entirely
3. cause pain for one's self and others
4. can be expressed in self-destructive ways and they can also be managed
5. are difficult to acknowledge
6. are taboo
7. can't be managed without acknowledgement.

According to Victoria, whiteness:

1. tries to repress chaos
2. is a part of you because of other people
3. is a universal concept
4. is associated with rules, little expression, detachment, a mold
5. often gives a sense of superiority
6. is privilege
7. is "normal."

According to Victoria, depression is:

1. chaos
2. a part of you because of who you are
3. not experienced by everyone
4. associated with art, critical thinking, creative expression
5. something that often makes you feel weak
6. discrimination
7. "abnormal."

At first, we wondered why we both had responded so viscerally to the diagram. (There was much to consider, so much insight from a brilliant young theorist of whiteness.) We began to talk about our experiences of growing up with parents who suffered from mental illnesses. We felt as though our parents' dis-eases[1] had differently situated us from other people we knew. We shared the sense that as middle-class white kids we were located more at the edges of whiteness than at its center. Victoria's insights were crucial for us to more deeply interpret our lives. They have helped us to think through how our whiteness might have been constructed in the not-yet-visible (to us) cracks in white supremacy. Lacking the right words, we could only explain ourselves as "messed-up." How we lived along the cracks and the edges, and what sorts of implications we can find for teacher-educators and teachers who take up race work, is what follows.

Jupp, Berry, and Lensmire (2016) have identified and called for research in a "second-wave critical whiteness studies." Their definitions are helpful:

> *Whiteness*, as definition, refers to hegemonic racial structuring of social and material realities operating in the present moment that perpetuate racialized inequalities and injustices. *White identity*, as definition, refers to the multiple, intersecting, and (often) race-evasive ways of conjugating White identity in the present moment. (italics in original, p. 4)

Important to us is how second-wave critical whiteness studies does not "totalize, reduce, or essentialize white identities" (p. 5). Therefore, it allowed us to consider our autobiographies as white people in more complex ways than a simple embodiment of privilege.

Yet even with complex theory it felt impossible to interrogate whiteness, to suggest that it is something less violent than it is. (There are so many ways for this to go wrong.) But we wonder if perhaps Thandeka (1999) was correct when she said that the very formation of our white identities necessitated a careful policing of anything that might disturb our internalized, inflexible ordering of racial reality. Perhaps such internal reference points for race exist so as *not* to permit either an analysis of our white identities or to resist what Thandeka (1999) described as the "lockstep discipline" of our whiteness. Said another way, white supremacy could be upheld when white identities are essentialized.

We addressed this chapter as a pedagogical project. We believe pedagogy requires us (all) to learn more about, and even trouble, concepts like whiteness and mental illness. It was, then, a pedagogical impulse—we wanted to learn more with Victoria as our teacher—with which we began to test the affordances and constraints of Victoria's theorizing in her Venn diagram. We, in a sense, have pieced together fragments of our white lives so that we could better understand our messed-up-ness as complexity. We see now how growing up with white, mentally ill parents shattered any sense of normal. We have lived what we are calling "abnormal" white lives.

We have paid serious attention to Victoria's theorizing, how she noticed that whiteness and depression share and don't share certain characteristics. Initially, we focused much of our writing and discussions on Victoria's insights into the similarities between whiteness and depression. Like other writers (see Logue, 2005; Morrison, 1992), Victoria's experiences led her to see such similarities.

But over time, we noticed—to our surprise—that we disagreed with several ways that Victoria characterized depression as *distinct from* whiteness, and that her way of noting their similarities did not capture all of our experiences either. In fact, the list of characteristics of depression named at least three ways we would describe our difficult white childhoods: chaotic, filled with weakness, and abnormal. Our sense of whiteness grew up out of living with parents who suffered from mental illnesses. We write about our childhoods to explore how our most difficult and memorable childhood stories contributed to our shared sense of not-fitting-in-the-world. Or, better said, not quite fitting in the white world.

In what follows, we briefly orient the reader to our families' histories, retell several stories from our childhoods, and interpret the ways in which our parents' mania, depression, and addiction enabled our own skepticism and critiques of whiteness and white supremacy. We contradict Victoria's distinction between depression and whiteness in three ways: 1) whiteness is not able to fully repress the chaos of being mentally ill or growing up with mentally ill parents; 2) children of parents suffering from mental illness do not feel superior to others; in fact, they are particularly weakened by their parents' ups and downs; and 3) families who suffer with mental illnesses weren't normal; in fact, they seemed and seem very "abnormal" in relation to the rest of the white community. Finally, we conclude by theorizing why and how such experiences may have contributed to our positioning as white teachers working for social justice and equity.

## DISTURBING WHITENESS (AUDREY)

First, Audrey introduces us to her family of origin through short autobiographical writing. Then, she explains what it felt like to be with her father when she was young through a narrative called "Selling Keys." Finally, she interprets the narratives with the help of Victoria's Venn diagram.

### The Very Short Story of Charles and Beatrice Fell Manaster

My parents were married in 1964. Mom worked as a first-grade teacher while Dad worked on a Masters of Business Administration (MBA) at the University of Chicago. I was born in 1968. Mom stopped teaching. Dad worked for a management-consulting firm. He was recruited to Boston, where we moved in 1970 or so. They built a house on a cul-de-sac in a new western suburb. My sister was born in 1972. That same year, Dad went on a business trip. Soon afterward his boss called Mom and told her to come to the airport. Dad had been sent home on a flight because he was talking nonsensically. He was immediately hospitalized. He was diagnosed with manic-depression. He lost his job. He found a new job and we moved to upstate New York. He lost his job. Mom divorced Dad. Mom and us girls moved to a Chicago suburb. He moved to Chicago. It was 1975.

## Selling Keys

My sister and I spent every other weekend of our childhood in Dad's roach-infested apartment with one chair and a mattress on the floor. He always told us soon he'd have another "high-powered" position but if those consulting jobs didn't come through he would work on his own company: "The Turn-around Fund of America" (TFOA). He talked and talked and talked. He called old rabbis and old professors to talk. He wrote many (fake) business memos. We organized and filed papers for our dad's (fake) businesses. My dad's mind was chaotic. When he was actually employed, he sold keys. We'd drive around the city of Chicago, eating McDonald's and going into old hardware stores with our dad who dressed in droopy polyester pants and a shirt covered with flakes from his psoriasis. We'd carry in a big black box filled with keys and we'd wait for him to fill the store's display rack.

## Whiteness as Chaos

I've thought a lot about my dad's life. He was born into a white, middle-class family with educated parents. He grew up attending elite public and private schools. He had a breakdown at age eighteen while away at college. It was covered up/forgotten/ignored. He married Mom. He had another breakdown. He couldn't hide anymore. He lived the rest of his life with the ups and downs of mania and depression.

Right before he and my mom divorced he was in a car accident. My mother bundled my little sister and me into the car to go to the scene. He had hit his head. The windshield was shattered. There were no airbags back then, so I suppose he was lucky to be alive. His gold Duster was totaled. For years after that accident, he would talk about it. He would repeat stories about it to me. In trying to understand, I guess I thought he had some kind of brain injury. That would explain the hospitalizations and my parents' divorce. I figured that the accident was why he talked and talked and talked and never made much sense. I realized much later it wasn't only a car crash that hurt my dad's head.

My "Selling Keys" story describes how my dad lived when I was in elementary school. I noted first the roaches because I was desperately afraid of them. There was only a little bit of furniture in the apartment. We helped Dad with an imaginary business. He told us about phone calls with important people. I knew, when we walked into places and talked to people, that he didn't make sense. I remember feeling ashamed. I remember that they tried to be nice to him and to us. My sister and I started calling him "weird." We didn't know how else to understand him.

We were two little white kids driving around with a weird white dad.

In the 1970s there were limited treatment options for someone diagnosed with manic depression.[2] Dad had been through shock therapy, hospitalizations, and different kinds of medications. He typically chose not to take his medication. It was impossible for me to separate out his personality from his illness. It was impossible to know if he was happy or manic. Later, when I was in college, he began to write me long, sometimes illegible, and disjointed letters. I didn't know when he was depressed. I knew he cared about me because he kept writing to me.

## Whiteness as Weakness

My dad's thinking, speaking, and writing could be characterized as a mess or perhaps as a dramatic inarticulateness (McDermott, 1988). Days and nights spent with him were chaotic and unpredictable because he was chaotic and unpredictable. There was no way to contain all of this. Victoria suggested that whiteness tries to repress chaos. Medication, hospitalization—those white and orderly ways of dealing with his dis-ease were attempts to repress the chaos. Dad may have wanted to, too. But he could not contain himself in the white way.

My dad, in manic episodes, exuded superiority. He told us he was smarter than the other businessmen he had known; he was stronger than the other high school swimmers he competed against; he was "healthy, wealthy, and wise" (his motto). In reality, Dad cried easily, slept little, was impatient and brooding, and suffered from an array of serious physical impairments, including diabetes. He seemed strong and weak and this made me feel confused, very small, and afraid. There was so little in my control. But I thought I had to be strong and responsible to take care of my dad and little sister.

Life with my white dad lay in such stark contrast to life with my white mom and her family. In my mom's community, white people had the social standing and wealth to support their feelings of superiority. I saw arrogance and ignorance. Mom had grown up in relative comfort. Her Jewish immigrant parents became wealthy small business owners and were beloved members of their all white (and almost all Christian) community. After the divorce from my dad, Mom wanted to return to the safety of her family. There we lived in a wealthy community—old money, big money, new money, flashy money. As I went back and forth between Dad's world and Mom's world from age seven into high school I became angry at the displays of wealth in Mom's community. I hated the big houses and the sports cars, the drugs and the clothes, the vacations, the inane competition, the snobbishness. These feelings were not only teenage rebellion but also the start of a sense of disgust at how the wealthy and white people in my community ignored the rest of the world—including my dad.

Mom happily occupied that white space. Dad—sick, poor, urban—was—how should I say it: cast out? I knew, from an early age, that there were different white worlds. I was tossed between the two.

## Whiteness as Abnormality

Victoria theorized that whiteness was "normal" and depression was "abnormal." Health is normal. Manic depression is not normal. Except when you grow up with a manic-depressive dad, that is your normal.

When Mom divorced Dad she told me it was because he was *sick*. Why was he sick? Could he get well?

In addition to the car accident explanation, my story about why Dad was sick went something like this: Dad was brilliant, Ivy League educated, and successful, but he pushed himself too hard and he broke.

I didn't want to get sick like him. I grew up telling myself I would not push myself too hard. One result of my dad's mental illness was that I learned that to be in my mom's community I was supposed to work at being wealthy. But I was afraid that if I did that, I would break like he did. Dad's fall, while in pursuit of success in business, sparked a skepticism of capitalism, consumerism, and competition. Dad's fall opened up questions about what it meant to be white.

When I was young, I was worried all the time. And the worriedness grew and grew and became my own experiences with depression and anxiety. I tried to hide all that inside. After all, my mother and her "normal" white community rejected my dad. It seemed as though my dad's mental instability and the conditions of his living were much too chaotic, too weak, too abnormal to be considered white. What would happen to me? Where did I fit in the white world?

## DISTURBING WHITENESS (SAM)

In what follows, Sam introduces us to his parents in a short vignette. Next, Sam shares an especially troubling memory he calls "Surviving Storms." Then he uses the same aspects—chaos, weakness, and abnormality—from Victoria's Venn diagram that Audrey called upon to make sense of his stories.

## Clayton and Wendy Tanner

My father Clayton's parents were Ukrainian Jewish immigrants. His grandfather was a merchant named David. David saved enough money to book passage to America during the Russian Revolution in 1917. Dad's grand-mother was killed trying to escape pogroms against Jews in the Ukraine. Dad's mother—my Bubbe—watched Cossacks shoot her mother in the head. Bubbe was eleven. Dad was raised in extreme poverty in St. Paul, Minnesota. Dad's father, also a Russian immigrant, changed his name from "Tankenov" to "Tanner." My mother Wendy was the daughter of Norwegian immigrants. Her parents were also poor. They were alcoholics. Mom began her struggle with bulimia at fourteen and became addicted to diet pills soon afterward. My father and mother met in the 1960s. What did they have in common? They liked to smoke pot. Dad became a zealous, Jew-for-Jesus freak soon after he met my mother. Mom and Dad were married in 1972. Mom lost three babies before her fourth was born four months early, resulting in my sister Christie's cerebral palsy. These pregnancies were difficult, in part, because of my mother's alcoholism and bulimia. I was born in 1980. My Hebrew name is Shmu'el, which means God listens. My parents believed that my healthy birth was divine. I was an answer to prayer. My father was unstable; he was bipolar, manic-depressive. Still, Dad was a gifted, charismatic insu-rance salesman. By the time I was born, Dad and Mom had purchased a house in an extremely wealthy, white neighborhood in the Twin Cities (Min-nesota). It would be seven years before alcohol, drugs, and their manic be-havior contributed to the dissolution of their marriage and, in turn, my child-hood.

## Surviving Storms

One night in 1987, soon before my parents' divorce, Dad left to buy pot from his dealer. I was seven years old. Mom was drinking wine coolers in the kitchen and grew convinced my father was with another woman. It had been raining all day, and a terrible thunderstorm had developed. I watched the wind toss the pine trees back and forth in our front yard. I was certain those trees would fall on our house. Mom told me she needed to find my father. I was worried my mother would get in a car accident, because I knew she was drunk. I demanded Mom take me with her. We left my older sister Christie in that big, Tudor house. The rain was intense, and visibility was limited. Mom hit a car near the gates to the University of St. Thomas on Cleveland Avenue. Her head slammed into the windshield. She had forgotten to buckle her seatbelt. I remember staring at her bloody forehead, speckled with glass. Mom was crying. I told her it would be okay. I *had* put my seatbelt on, and was fine. Dad arrived at the hospital around midnight. He was in a rage. Dad threatened to kill my mother for taking me into that storm. I remember standing in a hospital room with my parents, embarrassed as the nurses and doctors watched my family fight. I tried to calm my parents down. I told them we were okay. I knew that we weren't. None of us ever seemed to be *okay*.

Mom and Dad divorced soon after the car accident I describe above. My father won custody of my sister and me. Dad told us it was rare for a man to win custody, but that my mother was a mess. She was. Mom remarried another alcoholic soon after she divorced my father and spent the next twenty years drinking herself to death.

Mom was routinely admitted to hospitals due to her alcoholism. On multiple occasions, doctors told me that my mother had pickled her liver and wouldn't survive the night. But Mom always seemed to pull through, return home, and find another bottle of vodka. Her second husband shot himself in 2011. After years of keeping my distance from my mother, she became a part of my life again. I was granted power of attorney, took over her finances, and imagined a place for her in my life. My fiancée and I were going to move into her house and take care of her. Ultimately, I couldn't watch Mom kill herself with pain medication and alcohol. I decided not to move in with her, and she was placed in a nursing home. My mother refused to quit drinking. She died in 2015.

My mother charmed people when they met her. On the surface, Mom was a warm, inviting person. She was a witty, white woman. Appearances were deceiving. Mom's drinking and drug abuse inevitably embarrassed me in front of friends, girlfriends, or even in school. Worse, it destroyed any chance for my life to be *secure*. Being with Mom was unsafe—it was impossible to say what new trauma she would invite into my life. My mother was *not normal* and, if I wanted to be normal, I needed to stay away from her.

Like Mom, Dad loved me very much. Still, he couldn't control his manic emotions. Dad would scream at me for spilling a glass of milk and, five minutes later, hug me and weep about how sorry he was. I was never sure what mood my father would be in, so I learned to hide in my bedroom. I played Nintendo and read books and ignored the constant fights between my sister and Dad.

Dad's license to sell insurance was revoked soon after the divorce. He illegally replaced a customer's Medicare supplement. Dad couldn't make the payments on our house in the Twin Cities. Yes, he had become wealthy. But Dad didn't come from money. He didn't know how to handle it. We moved three times in three years. Eventually, my father settled in another affluent, white neighborhood in the suburbs. Dad didn't clean the house, do the laundry, buy me clothes, or cook dinner. I learned—to whatever degree I could— to take care of myself.

Eventually, Dad married a stern, evangelical Christian. Susan was white, and extremely unkind to me. During high school, I spent more and more time in the homes of my white, suburban friends. My father was a constant subject of conversation with my friends. They made fun of his custom license plate that read "Yeshua," which is the Hebrew word for Jesus. Dad looked like a regular, white person but, after my friends learned more about him, they made it a point to make fun of the ways that he was different from their white parents. This difference extended to me. My friends called me a short, Russian Jew, and teased me—sometimes warmly—about being different. I *was* different. My parents were different too. When Dad did meet my friends' parents or my teachers, he either told them about the gospel or tried to sell them insurance policies. I loved Dad, but was always embarrassed when he entered the white worlds of my childhood.

As was the case with Audrey and her stories above, white privilege can explain some of my upper-middle-class childhood.

Yet, my family wasn't *normal*. I worked hard to appear normal to teachers and friends, but always knew I wasn't like them. Yes, I am a white man. But my whiteness is abnormal and, like Audrey, was disturbed by my upbringing. I love my parents very much, and honor their gifts, even as I share these unpleasant histories. Dad was emotionally perceptive, and my mother was a creative force. Still, my desire to appear normal—perhaps to be perceived as white (in my behavior, as much as in the color of my skin)—required me to turn away from my parents, and, in that way, I always understood that being normal (or maybe being white) was false. It was an act for other people. It was fake.

It wasn't who I really was.

## Whiteness as Chaos and Weakness

Audrey used Victoria's claim that depression is chaos and that whiteness is the repression of chaos to understand her father. Certainly, time spent with my parents was also chaotic.

Was Dad going to yell at me for listening to my music too loudly? Was he going to get angry because I was hiding from him in my room? Would he come home at night before bed? Would he bring home groceries? Would he uproot us from another neighborhood and move me to another school? Every day with Dad was unstable—there was no way to predict his behavior. I learned to adapt and to brace for the unexpected. Was the chaos that I felt inside due, in part, to my father's behavior—to depression? I can't say for sure. Certainly, I often felt sad. I have countless childhood memories of sitting in my bedroom and crying, often for little reason other than my circumstances were overwhelmingly painful.

School and the homes of my friends in the upper-middle-class, white neighborhoods where I lived were not chaotic—things were organized, and their parents were reliable. But I knew that, in order to fit into their worlds, my father or mother could not be brought with me. Externally, I learned to behave like my normal, white friends. Internally, I repressed the great sadness that my family was different, that they were a mess. If whiteness is the repression of chaos, then I can understand my time with white friends, in white schools, and, ultimately, as a teacher in white institutions in terms of the repression of the things that are not welcome in tidy, white spaces.

Morton, Jackson, Frazier, and Fasching-Varner (2017) contend that schools are designed to serve white values and especially to privilege white men. Presumably, schools are designed to benefit me. But there were things about me, things born out of my childhood, that didn't fit in school and, therefore, I had to repress in order to access school. What were those things? My mother's alcoholism, her addictions, and her neglectful parenting were *bad*. My father's manic behavior, his Jewish heritage, and his evangelizing embarrassed me. Again, Mom and Dad were not welcome in the white worlds I was learning to inhabit, and I knew my inclusion in those worlds required their absence.

Like Audrey, my childhood prepared me to be skeptical of whiteness, even as I learned to fit into its machinations. I was unlike the white people who seemed to naturally inhabit white spaces—I knew I wasn't actually superior to anybody. I was different from these normal, white people. Still, I stopped talking about my mother and father. I spoke "proper" (white) English, wore expensive sweaters from Abercrombie & Fitch, and listened to Nirvana. I tried to be everything my white teachers and friends expected me to be.

## Whiteness as Abnormality

Audrey has already described how Victoria theorized that whiteness was "normal" and depression was "abnormal." I've pointed out the ways that my father and mother—and the depression I'm associating with living with their addictions and their manic behavior—became normal to me. My abnormal father and mother created the context for my childhood, and that childhood was, in some ways, normal, *to me*.

"Your family is really fucked up, Sam," my white friends would tell me in high school. They enjoyed teasing me about how neglectful my parents were. I'd laugh and agree with my friends. Still, my childhood had *felt* normal to me as it was happening.

My father took us to a synagogue on Saturday mornings and a different denomination of Christian church each Sunday. This was normal to me. Dad smoked too much pot and couldn't get out of bed. This was normal to me. My father was laughing warmly one moment and screaming at my sister Christie the next. I became accustomed to volatile mood swings. Dad belittled me one moment and told me he loved me the next. Dad was an enormous and—in relation to my friends' parents—abnormal presence in my life, and his abnormality became *my* normal during childhood.

My mother passed out on the couch during my visits to her house on the weekends. This was normal. Mom called me to tell me she was breaking up with my stepfather because he hit her while he was drinking. She called and told me she had a heart attack, even though she hadn't. I never knew if my mother was telling the truth—she often lied to win my sympathy or, at the least, my attention.

Ultimately, my parents' behavior (or my stories about my parents) always stood out in normal, white spaces. Teachers, doctors, and my friends raised their eyebrows when they met my parents or listened to my stories. I learned to avoid bringing up my parents, because they seemed unwelcome in white spaces.

I learned to behave in certain ways, as I realized I wouldn't be welcome either. I realized I shouldn't behave like my father did when I was in white spaces. If I mimicked Dad's sarcasm, his "Jewishness," and his volatile (and open) emotions, I'd get in trouble.

In my sixth year as a high school teacher, I was almost fired for "inappropriate" behavior. I was placed on two three-day suspensions and would have been fired if I hadn't already been tenured at a different high school. When pressed, the principal told me that I didn't act "professionally" enough. She told me I was sarcastic, too open with my students, and used offensive language. Just like Dad.

I had taught for four years at a high school with a predominately Black student population, before moving to this school where most students were white. Teaching at my first school was liberating. The students gravitated toward me, and I connected deeply with the same—mostly Black—students who gave my white colleagues trouble. Teaching at the second school was more difficult for me.

Ultimately, despite being named most inspirational teacher that sixth year, I was placed on the teacher-assistant track. Three other teachers were assigned to meet with me and to observe my teaching. I needed to prove that I was acting more appropriately, or I would be fired. The white administration tried to fix me, to make me behave more "appropriately," more "professionally," more "normally," and, perhaps, more whitely.

Indeed, I was explicitly told by my white administration that my behavior might have been okay at my previous school, but that my new school had higher expectations. I never knew what that actually meant, but always read the comment as having racial undertones.

I learned to behave in the ways white administrators at my second school wanted me to—I was less sarcastic, made sure never to swear, and avoided reading provocative material with my students. I didn't really *believe* in that behavior, but I wanted to keep my job. Was I learning to behave in affirmation of white, middle-class values? Perhaps that was part of it. And my behavior was becoming more of a performance. It wasn't real. I continued to be myself around my students. Students continued to name me the most inspirational teacher, and I hoped the principal wouldn't catch me being me.

## CONCLUSION

Why is it that of all of our childhood stories, our most vivid memories, were connected to car crashes and broken glass? Those moments were frightening, of course. But we noticed too that broken glass or shattered glass resonated deeply with our faith tradition. We recalled a Jewish creation myth that we learned as children in synagogue and at home. We were taught that when God created Earth, sparks of light were placed in vessels. When those vessels shattered it became the task of the Jewish people to gather up the slivers and to use them to repair a broken world. Our childhoods were similarly shattered. Not only did our parents suffer from profound mental illnesses, the larger wealthy and white communities where we were raised caused us to question traditional boundaries of whiteness. We were not, like the white people Thandeka (1999) interviewed, carefully policed to stay in our white communities.

In this chapter, we explored how Victoria's Venn diagram was a powerful tool for our thinking and writing about our experiences with mental illness and whiteness. Our shared sense of being "messed-up" followed us into our adult lives, our teaching, and our understanding of whiteness. Our careers as teachers grounded in our relationships with students of color enabled us to continue to question and reject white supremacy.

We close with a reflection on Sam's teaching because we believe we can learn from the interpretations of our childhood stories about why Sam (and Audrey and other white antiracist educators) was and remains a radically open teacher and how that might contribute positively to our antiracist projects.

Sam has never kept much from his students and willingly talks about any topic. He was, perhaps, the most open to Victoria. They talked openly about her feelings of depression and anxiety. It seemed to him, at the time, that Victoria needed somebody to listen to her without judgment and to help her to make sense of what was happening to her. Because he had experienced so much chaos with his parents' ways of living, Victoria's struggles did not seem small, not at all—but they were not frightening to Sam. They were normal.

In June of 2013, Victoria nonchalantly told Sam that working with him during her junior year in high school might have saved her. We believe Sam's capacity to listen to Victoria allowed her to make better sense of her anxiety as well as of race. He empathized with her and provided her avenues—through teaching and learning—to work with her feelings of messed-up-ness. Her Venn diagram is an example of that work.

Teaching and learning are about the reciprocal, complex interactions between people. Perhaps, in conceiving a second wave of critical whiteness pedagogy, we might start to wonder what teachers can learn from and with their students—especially their white students—about what whiteness is, and how it works.

## REFERENCES

Disease (n.). (n.d.). Retrieved October 16, 2017, from www.etymonline.come/word/disease
Jupp, J. C., Berry, T. R., & Lensmire, T. J. (2016). Second-wave white teacher identity studies: A review of white teacher identity literatures from 2004 through 2014. *Review of Educational Research, 86*(4), 1151-1191.
Lensmire, A. (2012). *White urban teachers: Stories of fear, violence, and desire.* Lanham, MD: Rowman & Littlefield.
Lensmire, A., & Schick, A. (2017). *(Re)narrating teacher identity: Telling truths and becoming teachers.* New York: Peter Lang Publishing.
Logue, J. (2005). Deconstructing privilege: A contrapuntal approach. *Philosophy of Education Archive,* 371-379.
McDermott, R. (1988). Inarticulateness. In D. Tannen (Ed.), *Linguistics in context: Connecting observation and understanding* (pp. 37- 67). Norwood, NJ: Ablex.
Morrison, T. (1992). *Playing in the dark: Whiteness and the literary imagination.* New York: Vintage.
Morton, B. C., Jackson, M. J., Frazier, M. E., & Fasching-Varner, K. J. (2017). Roadblock in the mirror: Recommendations for overcoming the cultural disability of whiteness in non-white educational spaces. In S. Hancock & C. Warren (Eds.), *White women's work: Examining the intersectionality of teaching, identity, and race* (pp. 3-17). Charlotte, NC: Information Age Publishing.
Tanner, S. (2016). Accounting for whiteness through collaborative fiction. *Research in Drama Education, 21*(2), 183-195.
Tanner, S. (2017a). Killing Victoria: Improvisational and emergent teaching and learning. *Ethnography and Education, 12*(3), 367-380. dx.doi.org/10.1080/17457823.2017.1287581.
Tanner, S. (2017b). Permission to be confused: Toward a second-wave of critical whiteness pedagogy. *Journal of Curriculum and Pedagogy, 14*(2), 164-179. dx.doi.org/10.1080/15505170.2017.1297745.
Thandeka. (1999). *Learning to be white: Money, race, and God in America.* New York: Continuum.

## NOTES

1. The choice to use a hyphen in the word dis-ease emphasizes the word's etymology and reminds the reader of our decisions to "Other" people who suffer such things. Dis-ease's Middle-English definition is "lack of ease; inconvenience" (disease, n.d.). We like how this use reminds the reader and ourselves that our parents experienced a "lack of ease" in their lives. We'll leave the reader to decide who experiences inconvenience.

2. In 1980 the American Psychiatric Association changed the name of manic depression to bi-polar disorder.

# Chapter Four

# The Colorblind Conundrum: Seeing and Not Seeing Color in White Rural Schools

Mary E. Lee-Nichols and Jessica Dockter Tierney

"I thought it was good. Now I hear it is bad?" "It" refers to colorblindness, and Ben was questioning his understanding of the term. This was part of Ben's apprehension regarding addressing race in his middle-level language arts classroom. Conflicting interpretations of colorblindness that surfaced in conversations with several teachers resonated with Mary, first author of this chapter and researcher in a larger study from which this and other examples are drawn.

Like many white people, Mary was inspired by Dr. Martin Luther King Jr.'s dream of a society in which the quality of a person's character is not assumed from the color of their skin. Learning about the Black Civil Rights Movement in middle school, Mary felt pride thinking that King's dream had actually been realized. In her white suburban existence, this was reinforced at an early age, as she learned from her parents that all people are equal, that the color of your skin means nothing. Jessie, a white woman and second author of this chapter, also grew up in a white suburban community. For her, examples of racial injustice only existed in history books and historical fiction, and equality and sameness were assumed as the contemporary norm.

Given our own upbringings, we (Mary and Jessie) recognize that many white people have interpreted King's vison to mean that they should not, under any circumstances, see race. And it makes sense that among those who embrace this ideology are teachers (Irvine, 2003; Lewis, 2001; Marx, 2006; McCarthy & Crichlow, 1993; Pollock, 2004; Sleeter, 1993; Vavrus, 2002) who would then be confused when a respected scholar such as Lisa Delpit (2007) asserts that "to not see race, is to not see children" (p. 159). But this chapter examines a peculiar form of confusion that occurs when teachers claim to quite *literally* not see race.

In her original study (Lee-Nichols, 2012), Mary engaged in conversations about race and diversity with ten white, rural, middle school teachers in predominantly white communities. The individuals with whom Mary spoke were generous and caring professionals, *and* they were caught up in the complicated consequences of a colorblind ideology that shaped the possible discourses available to them as they navigated both the absence and, at times, significant presence of racial diversity in their schools and communities. In this chapter, primarily through work with the story of a teacher, Lauren, supplemented by statements from Ben, June, and Ruth, we explore these white, rural teachers' uncertainty: the dilemma of whether to notice race in the classroom or other spaces, and the confusion articulated around color-blindness.

For us as scholars and teachers, these white teachers' claims to literally not see the race of individual students with whom they work is both unsettling and illuminating. While it is hard for us to believe that some white teachers did not recognize the race of students who were in their classrooms or on their teams, we draw upon their stories to attempt to make sense of such an extreme form of colorblindness and to link our analysis to an exploration of how the history of white dominance in the United States has impacted predominantly white classrooms and schools. Our purpose is to use the particular experiences of these rural, Midwestern, white teachers to better understand the complexities that exist within the larger phenomenon of colorblindness.

## COLORBLIND DISCOURSE AND COLORBLIND RACISM

Much has been written about colorblindness as a phenomenon in historical-legal, sociological, psychological, and educational terms. According to Eduardo Bonilla-Silva (2010), colorblind racism, which became a dominant framing for race in the late 1960s, differs from the Jim Crow racism that foregrounded a biological or moral inferiority of Black people (and other people of color). Instead, in colorblind racism,[1] whites rationalize the inferiority of people of color as the result of individual characteristics (e.g., laziness), natural tendencies (e.g., students of color not wanting to take honors courses), or market dynamics (e.g., some jobs as well-suited to certain groups of people). The result is the maintenance of a system that reproduces white supremacy in covert and institutionalized ways.

Classrooms and schools play a significant role in this reproduction of inequities through colorblind racism. The ideology and discourse through which colorblind racism operate (Beeman, 2015) allow white teachers (and students, administrators, and parents) to disregard the significance of the historical, social, cultural, and economic factors that shape the racialized experiences, past and present, of students of color (Chapman, 2013). Ignoring the significance of race allows white teachers to frame youth of color as individuals who, given what are perceived to be the same opportunities and access to classroom experiences, are simply too disinterested, unmotivated, or irrational to take advantage of them (Tarca, 2005). In other words, when schools and teachers do not see race, any "failure to achieve is therefore the fault of people of color themselves" (Frankenberg, 1993, p. 14).

Early studies of whiteness in education signaled a colorblind stance in teachers (Darling-Hammond & Bransford, 2005; Irvine, 2003; McCarthy & Crichlow, 1993; Marx, 2006; Schofield, 1989; Sleeter, 1993; Vavrus, 2002). For example, Amanda Lewis (2001) analyzed racial messages students received from teachers who took pride in their colorblind stance, saying that in their community race did not matter because everyone was treated the same. Denying the significance of race and framing racial discourses around sameness suggest the extent to which a colorblind ideology shapes the racial landscape for practicing teachers today.

Yet, at the same time, the political and rhetorical contexts of our country make it difficult for white teachers, and others, to know when and if it is "appropriate" to name race in the public domain. Legal scholar Ian Haney López (2006) writes that colorblindness is "a set of understandings—buttressed by law and the courts, and reinforcing racial patterns of white dominance—that define how people comprehend, rationalize, and act on race" (p. 62). Such understandings have developed through a difficult history surrounding race. In 1896 the U.S. Supreme Court case *Plessy v. Ferguson* deemed separate public accommodations constitutionally sound. Nearly sixty years later, the same court ruled in *Brown v. Board of Education of Topeka* that segregated educational institutions were indeed unconstitutional. In the late 1960s, civil rights leader Martin Luther King Jr. declared his dream for his children to be judged on the content of their character and not on the color of their skin, the misinterpretation of which led many to believe that living in a colorblind society was part of that dream. And more recently in the U.S. Supreme Court case, *Parents Involved in Community Schools v. Seattle School District No. 1* (2007), our country's highest court ruled it unconstitutional for school districts to racially balance school demographics because it was not a viable state interest (Han, 2015). In concluding his opinion for the plurality, Chief Justice Roberts wrote, "The way to stop discrimination on the basis of race is to stop discriminating on the basis of race" (PICS, 2007).

Such a context is central to the circulation of colorblind discourses and to the secure place of colorblind racism in U.S. schools and society. Roberts's assertion is, after all, the primary assertion of a colorblind racism: That the only way to end racial discrimination is to ignore race and to treat individuals as individuals (Tarca, 2005). In other words, to not see race is the only way to eliminate racism. As such, colorblind discourse "explains contemporary racial inequality as the outcome of nonracial dynamics" (Bonilla-Silva, 2010, p. 2). And yet, such discourse contributes to "new racism" (Bonilla-Silva, 2010), where racial inequities are hidden or "structured" in policies and practices that value sameness over difference. A colorblind racism, then, serves to conceal power structures built upon racial inequities and halts efforts to remake those structures (Haney López, 2007).

Within this context the motivations of white teachers who assert a colorblind ideology are ambivalent and complex. Often, such teachers deploy colorblind discourse to appear to lack bias and prejudice, to expound the value of a meritocratic system, and to remain polite. Their own whiteness and the colorblind discourses which frame them police the very possibilities for what white teachers can know, name, and be in relation to race (Morrison, 1992; Thandeka, 2001).

Within this body of literature on colorblind discourses and racism, there is limited discussion, however, of teachers who insist they *literally* do not see race. It was difficult for us to imagine that someone could not see differences that seem so apparent. Race is, in fact, a category into which people quickly and automatically place others (Montepare & Opeyo, 2002, as cited in Apfelbaum & Sommers, 2008). And yet, the teacher, Lauren, whose story we focus on in this chapter, claimed to *not see*—even after it was pointed out to her—the race of a Black student on her gymnastics team. A goal for this chapter, then, is to wonder about and explore how colorblindness, as a theoretical framework, stops short of helping us understand teachers for whom colorblind discourse may be both trying to say the right thing related to race (Winans, 2005) and perhaps to do something more. It is that something more we hope to unearth.

## TALKING ABOUT RACE IN THE RURAL MIDWEST

In her study, Mary interviewed rural, white teachers in the upper Midwest to better understand their experiences as they conveyed what it was like to encounter diversity and to talk about race in their primarily white schools and communities. These were schools in districts with fewer than 2500 residents, whose reported student population was between 92 and 98 percent white. In these schools, white teachers would likely have had a student of color at some point within three to four years and would have an experience with racial differences to narrate.

Conducting this study in rural communities meant seeking participants from a wide geographic area, and Mary sometimes traveled twenty to thirty miles between schools and up to 168 miles in one day. As she traveled to these rural communities, Mary was struck by the peaceful and quiet land-scape, writing in her study journal: "on the meandering country roads of the Midwest I was even more aware of the peace and the quiet nature of rural America. I wondered if the silence of racial discourse was deliberate, as if discussions of race would somehow disrupt this tranquil landscape." At other times, she witnessed the marks of a racist history on those same paths: "On the drive to his school earlier in the year I passed a parked pick-up truck that had two large confederate flags mounted on either side of the truck-bed and a farmhouse garden that had a lawn ornament statue of a Black boy fishing." Mary's reflections on the rural communities in which her participants lived capture both the silence and the alarming presence of race and racism that permeates the landscape and the teachers' stories.

Mary interviewed ten teachers who met the study criteria (i.e., rural white teachers who were willing to share their experience of talking about race). She asked participants to think of a time in the classroom when they engaged in a discussion about race or racial issues with students and to describe the setting. Some participants took a long time to get to the experience; they were hesitant to talk about it. But all did, and most with great clarity once they got started.

Teachers in this study articulated fear, discomfort, uncertainty, anger, frustration, experience, and paralysis in their responses and in their stories. In the next section, we turn to colorblind examples teachers shared with Mary.

## "I Didn't Even Realize It": Expressions of Colorblind Confusion

We begin our discussion with Lauren, a classroom guidance teacher and counselor for grades five through eight. She described a situation where, even upon having it pointed out, Lauren denied that one of the students she worked with was Black. Lauren was generous, enthusiastic, outgoing, and friendly. She eagerly approached Mary and became the first participant in her study. Lauren entered into discussions of race with the same energy, but also with great uncertainty. The following experience that Lauren describes took place while she was coaching a gymnastics meet:

> But I remember back when I was coaching—I tend to think I'm colorblind. And I guess here's an example. This must have been about 1992. I was coach-ing, and I had a gymnast on my team. And I love her dearly—still do—good gymnast of mine. And she came from—she was adopted into a white family. But that didn't even cross my mind—whether she was in a white family or a Black family. So anyway, I remember a coach coming up to me and saying, "Wow. That Black gymnast of yours is such a good vaulter. Wow." And I'm like, "What do you mean Black gymnast? I don't have a Black gymnast on my team." And he said, "Well, yes. You do have a Black gymnast on your team." I said, "No. I do not. I have twelve girls on my team. I do not have a Black

gymnast." I mean I argued with him probably three or four times. And all of a sudden, he pointed her out, and I'm like, "Oh wow. I do have a Black gymnast." I didn't even realize it. So in the back of my mind, with this incident, I began to think that I'm colorblind. Because I was taught to treat everybody the same by my parents—that I maybe didn't notice teaching or coaching people of a different race. In fact, sometimes when we do surveys here at school—we have to—you know for putting down our population—I have to really, really, really, really, really go through the list, or even look at a student, to notice that they're maybe Native American or maybe Asian-American.

A first possible interpretation of Lauren's not-seeing race in this instance is that she is engaging in the colorblind rhetoric that scholars like Ruth Frankenberg (1993) and Amy Winans (2005) shed light upon. Winans (2005), for example, suggested that white people might enact a colorblind stance to show that they are not racist and "as a sort of cover for 'hesitant and confused feelings concerning race'" (p. 262). These "hesitant and confused feelings concerning race" could play a part in Lauren's color evasion in the example here. Lauren felt uncertainty about when it was appropriate to see difference. As Frankenberg (1993) argued, white women perform colorblindness in response to the belief that to see color is bad and to not see it is good. These women, like Lauren, attempt to enact the identity of the good white person by remaining blind to race. Lauren is in a morally confusing position when confronted by actual difference, and a colorblind ideology is alluring because it appears the politically correct choice. As Frankenberg (1993) pointed out, however, such moves, while perhaps well intended, always preserve the power structures in place and work against antiracist change. As such, Lauren does not need to see race because her own position in a white supremacist society does not require that she notice or acknowledge it, particularly if the gymnast on her team, who may not have acted in ways Lauren viewed as culturally Black, figures into storylines framed by white ways of knowing and being in her rural community.

For us, the problem with this interpretation is *not* that it is inaccurate. Indeed, for Lauren, not seeing the race of the gymnast on her team signals to the other coach that she is somehow beyond seeing race, that the race of the gymnast, for whom she claims to care deeply, does not matter for that very reason. In this moment, then, Lauren tries to demonstrate to the other coach that she is a good white woman who sees people, not race. However, given Lauren's emphatic denial of racial difference in this moment ("I have twelve *girls* on my team"), this interpretation also feels incomplete; it does not account for the complex and contextual factors that influence Lauren's rhetoric.

This invocation of colorblind rhetoric may be, for example, what Jessica Vasquez (2014) refers to as an "optimistic" colorblindness, which signals that racial identifications do not hold Lauren back from having a deep and memorable relationship with this gymnast on her team. For Vasquez, "Color-blind rhetoric is not always inherently racist and invested in White dominance but can instead underscore similarity and be a basis for emotional bonds" (p. 283). Lauren makes a point of saying that she loves this gymnast dearly, and yet, she argues three or four times with another coach who identifies the gymnast as Black. For us, this signals something beyond merely wanting to say the right thing related to race; it signals Lauren's deep desire to construct her relationship with her Black student in a way that foregrounds a bond strengthened by what she has perceived, up to this point, as sameness. When a key difference is pointed out to Lauren—one that is apparent to any observer willing to name it—Lauren feels anger and resentment toward the individual who named this difference. Such resentment may stem from the direct contradiction between a belief in her white community by which Lauren has lived—that everyone is the same and she must treat them as such—and the reality that she "loves dearly" someone now openly categorized as different. A love framed by difference opens Lauren to the possible loss of her white community (Thandeka, 2001) or the loss of her relationship with a beloved student—losses which, until race was named, Lauren had not faced.

We offer, next, another possible, complex, interpretation: that rural teachers like Lauren strategically use colorblind rhetoric in an attempt to protect students of color from harmful, oppressive stereotypes and discourses circulating in the communities in which they live and teach. This perspective, which considers observations participants made about the significance of community in shaping racial discourse, points to a notion white teachers may hold—that in predominantly white communities, students of color are somehow safer if no one notices difference. We draw on comments from another white teacher, Ben, to illustrate this point.

Ben, a language arts teacher, was ever conscious of messages he might be unconsciously sending to students, especially those that might conflict with ideas students may have received outside of school. He shared troubling discourse he encountered in the community that made it difficult for him to speak of racism in a historical sense, when racist sentiment was still present in conversations he had with parents of the students he teaches:

> The hard part is when there's people outside the school that are speaking differently on how to treat minorities and if the students get influence from someone else in the community or their relatives. . . . I'm aware of some of the parents and some of the relatives of students that I've taught and their comments are sometimes not as polite as they should be.

Though he hesitated and did not elaborate on the language, the images that Mary observed while driving through rural communities, as we shared earlier, supported what he was suggesting. Loretta Brunious (1998) described such artifacts as having "spawned negative images and dehumanizing stereotypes of blacks in America that refuse to be dislodged even today . . . These images have contributed to a subconscious acceptance of inferiority and the stubborn persistence of racism today" (p. 22). Prior to her study Mary also recalled a local newspaper featuring a front-page article about Homecoming activities that included a photograph of royalty candidates, two of whom were wearing blackface makeup and Afro wigs from a Homecoming skit performed for the school. The article was solely about Homecoming activities—that students were in blackface was not recognized as racist by students, parents, administrators, or the media that covered the event. When Mary questioned the school administration about this, she was told that no disrespect was intended; it was simply students dressing up as The Jackson Five for a skit.

Understanding the context of such communities, when Lauren claims she cannot racially identify the lone student of color in her school and Ben expresses concern about racist influences outside his school, these white teachers enlist a colorblind rhetoric, which has been structured by their communities, as a move to protect students of color from racist associations. Following her interview, Lauren made this comment, "Now that I think about it, was I trying to prove my point? I was angry that he [the other coach] classified her—that he identified her because of her race." At this moment, Lauren hints at a complex motive for her colorblind rhetoric. Her *anger* at the categorization of one of her gymnasts as Black signals that Lauren not only sees race, but that she works on a conscious level to avoid naming it: "I argued with him probably three or four times." Such an interpretation suggests that if Lauren's student is classified as Black—a categorization with a primarily negative association in her community—her student is open to the racist rationalizations of inferiority and dehumanizing stereotypes put upon people of color and may even become a target for discrimination and hatred. Lauren rejects what feels like a racist categorization for her student. In arguing away the classification of "Black" for this gymnast, Lauren protects herself and her Black student from a surrounding community that has demonstrated the "stubborn resistance" of racism lodged within it.

Lauren was not the only teacher in the study to literally fail to see race. While her refusal to accept a racial identifier for a gymnast on her team was the most notable and puzzling denial of color, Ruth, another teacher, could not readily identify students of color in her classroom, even though they were present, and June could not recall for sure if she had ever had a Black student. This general uncertainty about and blindness to race surfaced throughout interviews with rural teachers in Mary's study, particularly in language associated with racial discourse. It was common for participants to stop mid-interview and ask if a term they were using was acceptable, often questioning how they were expressing themselves. For example, describing a book used in his class, Ben stated, "I was probably more nervous and more sensitive just making sure that I was proper, and then even the choice of—is it African American? Is it Black? I've noticed you've said African American."

This uncertainty and stumbling around racial language revealed two concerns framed by a fear that often prevented teachers from bringing up race at all. First, teachers were fearful that what they were saying was either politically incorrect, offensive, or inaccurate, and therefore racist. Second, and of greatest concern, was fear of causing a student of color to feel badly if what they *do* say is received as offensive or inaccurate. Indeed, Ben described discussing race with his class and recalled how he was conscious of avoiding eye-contact with the one student of color in the room, even as he kept glancing at the student because he wanted to make sure the student was okay with what was being said. And at the same time, he continually scanned the room to see if other students were looking at that classmate. This gave Mary the sense that Ben and other white teachers who spoke of similar experiences were also challenging their students not to see race; even though they were talking about race, they did not want their white students to notice that there was a student of color in the classroom or to recognize that what the teacher was saying about race had anything to do with a classmate of color.

In these examples of overtly not seeing or deliberately trying not to notice race, colorblind discourses serve a policing role. That is, the very language that these white teachers have available to them to name their questions and observations around race—or even more, to teach their students about the material consequences of race in the United States—is controlled and patrolled by colorblind ideologies and the discourses that circulate in and through them. By fearing that they might get things wrong and harm the students of color in their classrooms, these white teachers are always already made as confused, uncertain, or, worst of all, racist by the discourses available for talking about race in their communities.

The examples of Lauren, along with Ruth, June, and Ben, suggest that rural white teachers adopt a colorblind stance within uncertainty and confusion about what is/isn't racist within the surrounding community and school. One teacher can, for example, readily identify racist discourse in the community outside of the school, but that five students appear in blackface within the school seems to go without question by teachers, administrators, or students. Within this contextual and conflictual landscape, Lauren, whose example of colorblindness is most literal and impactful due to the tenacity with which she refused to see race, enlists colorblind rhetoric in relationship to multiple and complex desires—to optimistically align her emotional bonds with a student of color, to defend and protect her from racist attitudes and institutions, and to get things "right" in discourses related to race. And yet, despite their intentions, the colorblind confusion of teachers like Lauren continues to contribute to white dominance in school spaces.

## THE RURAL CONTEXT

The stories of Lauren, Ben, Ruth, and June demonstrate the tensions around whiteness and the mostly white contexts within which they live. Their identities as white people and white teachers are shaped by larger racialized discourses that both construct and obstruct possible ways of being white in their local communities. This is significant in rural contexts where the majority of teachers earn their undergraduate degrees from colleges within 150 miles of their home *and* find teaching positions within that same radius (National Center for Education Information, 2005). For some rural communities, there exists a likelihood, then, that teachers' life and college experiences may be within predominantly white communities. For many white teachers, the white settings in which they were educated and raised serve as influential sites in which they construct racial identity and attitudes surrounding race. In this section, we offer three viewpoints on white teachers working in the influential sites of predominantly white, rural communities.

First, within rural sites, colorblindness is a dominant discourse, one that acts on and through white teachers like those whose stories we share in this chapter. Colorblind discourses shape the words, silences, and very ways in which Lauren, Ruth, June, and Ben see and do not see in the world. Those discourses inform their white racial identities at the same time that they must navigate them, attempt to make sense of them in their interactions around race, and ultimately, make messes with them. In a way, rural white teachers working in predominantly white communities are doomed to fail at race when the available (colorblind) discourses police their words and actions while also blaming them for their failure.

Second, within white rural communities, white teachers draw upon a colorblind ideology, as Timothy Lensmire (2014) argues, to avoid and manage conflict with other white people. We see Lauren's colorblindness, in this way, as a possible move to prevent ruptures around race within her white community. When the other coach calls out race as a significant marker of difference, Lauren's anger may be both protective of the Black gymnast on her team and anger at the rupture this moment creates. She cannot name the reasons for her own anger, but for us, her desire to have a close relationship with the young woman stands in tension with a member of her white community calling out, in a way, Lauren's lack of knowledge or comfort with race. Lauren is safe in her whiteness only when she need not fully confront it (Matias, 2015). As such, moments where race is named, called out, or made present disrupt the racial tranquility—that is, the white supremacy—of rural landscapes.

The final viewpoint we offer is that white teachers are in constant conflict around race even as they are, sometimes strategically, sometimes ignorantly, blind to it. That conflict is one constantly oriented to discourses that determine, limit, and police the possible ways of being white in interaction with people of color in the world. The dominant discourse available to white teachers in rural, white communities is a colorblind ideology, one that suggests to them that good white people do not, should not, and ultimately cannot see race.

Fear, discomfort, and uncertainty seem inexorably linked, moving white teachers toward a paralysis that threatens to silence discussions of race and settle into the relative ease, for white social actors, of living in a state of colorblindness. The colorblind conundrum becomes a connection between the inherent goodness of caring teachers wanting to do what is best for their students and making a choice that is well-intentioned, yet uninformed and ultimately supportive of racist structures already in place. Reinforcing and perpetuating a colorblind perspective has enduring negative effects for both students of color and white students. Instead, we must emphasize the importance of giving teachers and students the support to understand and develop identities that would allow them to challenge damaging ideas of racial superiority and privilege rather than fostering either negative beliefs and stereotypes, or colorblind stances (Derman-Sparks, Ramsey, & Edwards, 2006).

Notably, Mary also found teachers who *were* able to move beyond their paralysis, and while they continued to experience discomfort related to race, they felt a responsibility as a teacher to move forward—for the greater good of being honest about race with and for their students. These teachers illuminated how challenging their fears and working within uncertainty allowed them to acquire the knowledge and experience that enabled them to see, acknowledge, and value the historical, present, and ongoing significance of race and race consciousness in their own and in their students' lives. We consider this working in and through uncertainty and complexity to be essential in nuancing, and ultimately resisting, a colorblind stance. The exploration of colorblindness we offer here has, we hope, highlighted the need for ongoing conversations focused on race to come to better understandings of the complexities of colorblind ideology, whiteness, and racism.

## REFERENCES

Apfelbaum, E., & Sommers, S. (2008). Seeing race and seeming racist?: Evaluating strategic colorblindness in social interaction. *Journal of Personality and Social Psychology, 95*(4), 918-932.

Beeman, A. (2015). Walk the walk but don't talk the talk: The strategic use of color-blind ideology in an interracial social movement organization. *Sociological Forum, 30*(1), 127-147.

Bonilla-Silva, E. (2010). *Racism without racists: Color-blind racism and the persistence of racial inequality in the United States* (3rd Ed.). Lanham, MD: Rowman & Littlefield Publishers, Inc.

Brunious, L. J. (1998). *How Black adolescents socially construct reality: Listen, do you hear what I hear?* New York: Garland Publishing.

Chapman, T. (2013). You can't erase race!: Using CRT to explain the presence of racism in majority white suburban schools. *Discourse: Studies in the Cultural Politics of Education, 34*(4), 611-627.

Darling-Hammond, L., & Bransford, J. (Eds.). (2005). *Preparing teachers for a changing world: What teachers should learn and be able to do.* San Francisco, CA: Jossey-Bass.

Delpit, L. (2007). Seeing color. In W. Au, B. Bigelow, & S. Karp (Eds.), *Rethinking our classrooms: Teaching for equity and justice, Volume 1* (Rev. Ed., pp. 158-160). Milwaukee, WI: Rethinking Schools.

Derman-Sparks, L., Ramsey, P. G., & Edwards, J. O. (2006). *What if all the kids are white?: Anti-bias multicultural education with young children and families.* New York: Teachers College Press.

Frankenberg, R. (1993). *White women, race matters: The social construction of whiteness.* Minneapolis, MN: University of Minnesota Press.

Han, S. Y. (2015). *Letters of the law: Race and the fantasy of colorblindness in American law.* Stanford, CA: Stanford University Press.

Haney López, I. (2006). Colorblind to the reality of race in America. *The Chronicle Review, 53*(11), B6.

Haney López, I. (2007). "A nation of minorities": Race, ethnicity, and reactionary colorblindness. *Stanford Law Review, 59*(4), 985-1063.

Irvine, J. J. (2003). *Educating teachers for diversity: Seeing with a cultural eye.* New York: Teachers College Press.

Lee-Nichols, M. E. (2012). Racial discourse in predominantly white classrooms: A phenomenological study of teachers' lived experiences discussing race. Unpublished doctoral dissertation, University of Minnesota, Minneapolis, MN.

Lensmire, T. J. (2014). White men's racial others. *Teachers College Record, 116*(3), 1-32.

Lewis, A. E. (2001). There is no "race" in the schoolyard: Colorblind ideology in an (almost) all-white school. *American Educational Research Journal, 38*(4), 781-811.

Marx, X. (2006). *Revealing the invisible: Confronting passive racism in teacher education.* New York: Routledge.

Matias, C. E. (2015). White skin, Black friend: A Fanonian application to theorize racial fetish in teacher education. *Educational Philosophy and Theory, 48*(3), 221-236.

McCarthy, C., & Crichlow, W. (Eds). (1993). *Race, identity, and representation in education.* New York: Routledge.

Morrison, T. (1992). *Playing in the dark: Whiteness and the literary imagination.* Cambridge, MA: Harvard University Press.

National Center for Education Information. (2005). Profile of teachers in the U.S. Retrieved from www.ncei.com/POT05PRESSREL3.htm.

Parents Involved in Community Schools (PICS) v. Seattle School District No. 1, 551 U.S. 701, 2007.

Pollock, M. (2004). *Colormute: Race talk dilemmas in an American school.* Princeton, NJ: Princeton University Press.

Schofield, J. W. (1989). *Black and White in school: Trust, tension, or tolerance?* New York: Teachers College Press.

Sleeter, C. (1993). How white teachers construct race. In C. McCarthy & W. Crichlow (Eds.), *Race, identity, and representation in education* (pp. 157-171). New York: Routledge.

Tarca, K. (2005). Colorblind in control: The risks of resisting difference amid demographic change. *Educational Studies, 38*(2), 99-120.

Thandeka. (2001). *Learning to be white: Money, race, and God in America.* New York: Continuum.

Vasquez, J. M. (2014). Race cognizance and colorblindness: Effects of Latino/Non- Hispanic White intermarriage. *Du Bois Review, 11*(2), 273-293.

Vavrus, M. (2002). *Transforming the multicultural education of teachers: Theory, research, and practice.* New York: Teachers College Press.

Winans, A. E. (2005). Local pedagogies and race: Interrogating white safety in the rural college classroom. *College English, 67*(3), 253-273.

## NOTE

1. Bonilla-Silva is careful to distinguish colorblind racism from colorblind ideologies. For the purposes of this chapter, we use both terms to connote the process by which white teachers evade, ignore, and outright deny the existence and significance of racial difference in their classrooms and schools.

*Chapter Five*

# A White Principal, a Fantasy of Dirt, and Anxieties of Attraction

## Bryan Davis and Timothy J. Lensmire

When was the first time you knew that race mattered? My (Bryan's) white father, Jim, was a nineteen year-old freshman at a state university in the Midwest in the fall of 1969. He had grown up in a small, mostly-white town and was a sociable person who became friends easily with new people he met. A couple months into his college experience he met Ben, an African-American student in the same dormitory. The two became good friends and went, on occasion, to weekend parties together. The racial makeup of these parties was usually about as racially diverse as the university as a whole—that is, not much, as almost everyone there was white.

One night, Ben and Jim were out and Ben said that there was a party he wanted to check out, so Jim went with him to a house party at an address they had not been to before. Forty years later, when my father told me the story, he remembered vividly how it felt to walk into the house and realize he was the only white person at a party with twenty or so African-American students. He instantly felt fearful, anxious, and uncomfortable. Ben turned and smiled at Jim and said, "It's a little different, huh?"

Ben had turned the tables on Jim in a humorous, yet meaningful, way. They only stayed at the party about an hour that night, but it is something that Jim never forgot. At that moment, race was powerful and meaningful to him on a personal level. Feelings of anxiety and discomfort flooded him based on nineteen years of being told by his white community, directly and indirectly, that African Americans were to be feared.

Unfortunately, my father's racial experiences as a young man still ring true today. Most white people in the United States lead segregated lives and grow up with little meaningful experience with people of different races.

This includes principals in our nation's schools. According to the National Center for Education Statistics (2016), 80 percent of public school principals in 2011-12 identified as white. These principals wield significant power in schools that are becoming increasingly racially diverse. Too often, these white principals are participating in decisions and practices that jeopardize educational opportunities for students of color, including in their role as the final authority on discipline, suspensions, and expulsions. And, as Tim and I explore in this chapter, they are making these decisions and framing policy with little understanding not only of the students and families of color with whom they work, but also with little insight into themselves—their own motivations, fears, desires—as white people, as racial actors in schools.

Drawn from a larger study with white administrators, this chapter focuses on a story that Meghan, a white high school principal, told about a racial experience she had when she was a high school student. Meghan said that she first realized that Black and white people were different when she gave her friend, Bob, who was Black, a ride in her car and thought that he smelled differently than a white person would.

We develop two different interpretations or readings of Meghan's story, and argue that what seems a fairly straightforward example of racist thinking and feeling is actually *both* such an example *and* something more complicated and telling. In the first reading, we examine how Meghan vacillated across at least two (and possibly three) different ways of understanding differences among Black and white people. One of these ways was what sociologist Ruth Frankenberg (1993) would call "essentialist racism" in that it located racial difference in biology. And given the importance of smell in Meghan's story, we also consider what psychiatrist and social critic Joel Kovel (1970) described as a *fantasy about dirt*—a fantasy that he thought was a significant part of white people's racial thought and feeling.

In our second reading of Meghan's story, Tim and I note that she claimed that Bob had been her friend since middle school, but that it was not until high school—and specifically, it was not until she was alone with him in a car and noticed that he was sweating and how he smelled—that she paid attention to the fact that he was Black and she was white. We argue that being close to and becoming aware of Bob's body aroused anxieties for Meghan that she was violating (or wanted to violate) prohibitions against her being with a young Black man.

In what follows, I first narrate an account of the larger study from which Meghan's story was drawn. Then, we discuss some of the analyses of race in the United States that informed our work to explore the meanings and significance of Meghan's story. Our goal is to enhance our understandings of who white administrators are and how to help them learn what they need to learn, so they can act powerfully against white supremacy and for racial justice within schools.

## BACKGROUND

### The Larger Study

My study examined six white administrators' experiences with race and how they made meaning of their whiteness (see Davis, 2011). I was one of the participants, along with five other white high school administrators from the same large high school in Wisconsin. All of us had been born, raised, and educated in white communities in the Midwest. And all of us had administrative experience in schools where the student population was becoming increasingly racially diverse.

Initial interviews with individual administrators included questions about where they had grown up, what they thought being white meant, experiences they had had in which race mattered, and how they thought race influenced the workings of their schools. Then, across three focus group meetings, we discussed Peggy McIntosh's (1988) concept of white privilege, examined a school poster for how it expressed white privilege, and explored Janet Helms's (2007) model of racial identity development. Final interviews focused on exploring ways that participants' ideas had changed and stayed the same across our conversations and work together in the interviews and focus groups.

For this chapter, Tim and I focused on a story that Meghan told me in her first interview. At the time of the interview, Meghan was a forty year-old associate principal. She had grown up in a small, white community and had had few experiences interacting with people of color as a child. She shared the story about being in the car with her friend, Bob, when I asked her to tell me about the first time she realized she was white or about an early experience in which being white mattered.

### Some Analyses of Race

For our chapter, Frankenberg's (1993) [1] account of the "evolving history of discourses on race difference" (p. 13) in the United States, as well as the Reverend Thandeka's (2001) and sociologist Katerina Deliovsky's (2010) analyses of how the desires of white women for people of color are policed and punished, are of particular importance.

Frankenberg (1993) thought that there were three primary ways that racial differences have been understood in the United States. The first, which Frankenberg named *essentialist racism*, imagines racial differences in "hierarchical terms of essential, biological inequality" (p. 14). She described the second primary discourse of race difference—*colorblindness*—in terms of a "double move toward 'color evasiveness' and 'power evasiveness'" and noted that, within this discourse, we are all the same under the skin; that, culturally, we are converging; that, materially, we have the same chances in U.S. society; and that—the sting in the tail—any failure to achieve is therefore the fault of people of color themselves. (p. 14)

For Frankenberg, the third discourse, *race cognizance*, contrasts sharply with colorblindness and its emphasis on sameness by insisting again on difference (as with essentialist racism). However, in this third discourse—which Frankenberg linked to radical antiracist and cultural nationalist movements in the late 1960s and early 1970s—racial difference signals, not the biological inferiority of people of color, but the "autonomy of culture, values, aesthetic standards, and so on. And, of course, inequality refers not to ascribed characteristics, but to the social structure" (pp. 14, 15).

Although Frankenberg represented these three discourses as emerging at different moments in history, she emphasized that they should not be interpreted as somehow replacing each other, in succession. Frankenberg would agree with sociologist Eduardo Bonilla-Silva's (2001) claim that a colorblind ideology has replaced an older, essentialist racist one as *the* dominant racial ideology in the United States. But Frankenberg would also argue that essentialist and race cognizant discourses haven't disappeared. Instead, they remain available to white people, along with colorblindness, as sources of thought and feeling about race. Our first reading of Meghan's story illuminates exactly the sort of mixture and conflict of different discourses that one might predict from Frankenberg's account.

Our second reading of Meghan's story, in contrast, focuses on anxieties and dangers that attended Meghan being *close* to Bob. Thandeka's (2001) portrayal of how white racial identities are constructed is helpful here. Thandeka, drawing both on psychoanalytic theory and historical work on whiteness and social class, argued that white selves are built out of the racial abuse, by white adults, of their own children and youth. That is, white children's desires do not, in the beginning, recognize the racial boundaries and hierarchies of our society. But soon enough, white children are confronted by adult disapproval that suggests that desires for friendship and love that point outside the white community are somehow wrong, and that if the child persists in pursuing such desires, then adult support and love may be withheld. Within such social dynamics, "good" white children are those who are furthest away from, who separate themselves from, people of color. The result, for Thandeka, was a white racial identity riddled with shame and ambivalence—a white racial identity defined by a desire to reach out beyond the white community and a deep confusion about, and fear of, this wanting.[2]

Deliovsky's (2010) interview study with twenty-four Canadian white women emphasizes that none of what Thandeka described was somehow over when white girls become white women. That is, white women's desires for friendship and love that point outside the white community are discouraged and disciplined. Locating white women's racial identities within the long history of European and North American white male patriarchy—and within its ongoing demand that white women's bodies only be accessible to white men, as part of the effort to reproduce a pure white race—Deliovsky documented how a

> gendered "white" identity is one that is engaged daily and incessantly (sometimes with anxiety and under duress) . . . women whom I interviewed who did not conform to the normative expectations around the performance of "white" feminine sexuality were accordingly reminded of their indiscretions through being called "white slut" and "nigger lover" and being subjected to other intragroup rituals whose function is to "put them back in their place." (pp. 72-74)

Our second reading of Meghan's story very much attends to whether or not Meghan, as a white female teenager, thought that she was in the right place when she was in that car, alone, with Bob.

## DISCOURSE AND RACE MIXING: TWO READINGS

We have rendered Meghan's story, below, in four paragraphs, to make it easier for us to refer to different parts of her account in the interpretations that follow.

### Meghan's Story

I remember the first time being white in a situation mattered. I had mentioned my friend Bob from middle school. Bob was, was Black, but I hadn't really noticed he was Black until one day in high school. He was on the hockey team. And I was the manager. And he forgot something at home. And so, I quick rushed him home.

And the interesting thing is I noticed he smelled differently. And so my first thought is, well, do all Black people smell differently? Because he's—he was sweaty. But, it was like a sweet smell. And so then I thought oh, my gosh—you're Black. And Black people smell differently when they sweat. And—and that was the first time I thought, oh my—you know there is really a difference here. It just made me realize that there is a difference here.

And I know that—some people say that, that race shouldn't matter. And some people say that race should matter and you should be proud of your race. But, I hadn't thought about the differences until there, when there was actually a physical smell. You know, yes—our skins are different. But I hadn't thought about that—it was just that smell that I will always remember. That—that that's how he was different.

And—and—and that was the only time. Then, still to this day, I don't notice that much of a difference. And I don't know if that's a good thing or a bad thing. But so far, it's worked for me.

## First Reading

This reading of Meghan's story focuses on three aspects: how Bob was treated by Meghan in the story as a member of a group, not as an individual; how Meghan assumed that Bob's "sweet smell" pointed to biological race difference; and how Meghan oriented herself toward varying discourses of race difference.

We begin by noting that, in the first two paragraphs of Meghan's story, Bob *became* a Black person for Meghan, seemingly for the first time. Meghan claimed that Bob had been her friend since middle school, but she "hadn't really noticed he was Black" until this moment. On the one hand, this distinguished or individuated Bob from the background of her classmates, who were almost all white. On the other hand, this also submerged Bob into blackness, as he shifted from being Meghan's friend to a representative of his race.[3]

When Meghan noticed what she described as Bob's "sweet smell," her "first thought" was "well, do all Black people smell differently?" It doesn't seem like this was an actual question for Meghan. She did not wonder if Bob used a different soap or antiperspirant or cologne or hair product than she was used to. Very quickly, Bob's smell was attributed to his being Black.

More significantly, this difference in smell was attributed to biological differences. Meghan left no doubt about this: "Black people smell differently when they sweat . . . our [Black people's and white people's] skin is different." The leap of thought, here, is from a difference in skin color being used as evidence, by Meghan, of a fundamental difference in our bodies, such that Black people and white people, in some deep way that transcends skin color, have *literally different bodies, different skins.* As Megan said, "you know there is really a difference here. It just made me realize that there is a difference here." This is a key way that essentialist racism works—by attempting to persuade us that something fundamental, something deep, can be intuited about others from the color (and smell) of their skin, from their surface.

In this case, Meghan connected difference not just to the color of Bob's skin, but also to how she thought he smelled when he sweated. With its focus on smell and sweat, Meghan's story participated in and drew upon what Kovel (1970) discussed as a powerful fantasy that "enters directly into aversive behavior" and that is associated with "that peculiar abstraction called dirt" (p. 81). A careful exposition of Kovel's analysis of dirt, grounded in psychoanalytic theory, would require more space than we have here. Luckily, such a rendering is unnecessary for suggesting how a fantasy of dirt functions within the white racial imaginary. Kovel wrote that:

> Every group which has been the object of prejudice has at some time been designated by the prejudiced group as dirty or smelly or both. . . . The English upper classes regarded the English middle and lower classes as dirty . . . and if the lower classes had "Untouchables," as in India, they would have doubtless exercised the same privilege over the lowliest as did the various castes within Indian culture. Indeed, lowest in social scale connotes the idea of dirtiest and smelliest, and untouchability sums up all these concepts in the framework of aversion. (pp. 81, 82)

Meghan asserted a biological race difference based on smell. And although she did not seem to express, here, any particular distaste for Bob's smell, her story participated in a powerful fantasy about dirt that links being dirty and smelly with lower positions in social hierarchies and that encourages white people to turn away from and separate themselves from Black people.

That said, this essentialist racism discourse was not the only one at play in her story.

Especially in the third paragraph, Meghan seemed to be sorting through different ways of thinking about or approaching race difference. She first invoked a colorblind discourse, saying that "some people say that, that race shouldn't matter." Then, she opposed this discourse to one in which race difference should matter: "And some people say that race should matter and you should be proud of your race." It is difficult to tell, from what she said here, whether "some people" referred to the sorts of antiracist and cultural nationalist activists Frankenberg associated with a progressive race cognizance discourse, or to white supremacists invoking an essentialist racism and demanding that white people "should be proud of your race." It was at this point that Meghan then asserted biological differences between Black and white people, as evidenced, for her, in the different smells different races make when they sweat.

Meghan's story, as a whole, can be read as being framed, book-ended, by a colorblind discourse. She began the story by saying that she "hadn't really noticed [Bob] was Black until one day in high school." And then—after invoking at least two and possibly three discourses of race difference in the third paragraph (depending on whether you believe "race should matter and you should be proud of your race" cited a race cognizance discourse or an essentialist racism one)—she seemed to settle at the end, once again, on a colorblind stance. (And this after asserting quite clearly that she believed Black and white people were biologically different.)

An effect of this framing in colorblind discourse is that Meghan's noticing of Bob's smell (and her noticing of what she took to be a biological difference) was uncommon, almost an aberration. She concluded her story thusly: "And—and—and that was the only time. Then, still to this day, I don't notice that much of a difference. And I don't know if that's a good thing or a bad thing. But so far, it's worked for me."

One moral to draw from Meghan's story is that her racial consciousness was characterized by the sort of "fault line or contradiction" that Frankenberg (1993) documented and theorized in her own interview study with white women. Frankenberg thought that a dominant colorblindness discourse created problems for her research participants, for these women knew that, in the real world, race mattered. She wrote that

> These women's efforts to "not see" race difference despite its continued salience in society and in their own lives generated a fault line or contradiction in their consciousness. . . . the women I interviewed grappled with and tried to pacify the contradiction between a society structured in dominance and the desire to see society only in terms of universal sameness and individual difference. The peace was an uneasy one, however, always on the brink of being disturbed. (p. 149)

Clearly, Meghan's experience with Bob in her car disturbed her easy embrace of a colorblind discourse. In making sense of the experience, she also drew on an essentialist racism discourse that posited biological race difference and that included a fantasy about dirt and social hierarchy. In our next reading of Meghan's story, we explore how it was not only an uneasy mixing of discourses that disturbed Meghan's peace of mind, but also anxieties and dangers associated with race mixing.

## Second Reading

If the conflict that drove our first reading was among different, opposing discourses of race difference, in this reading the conflict is among generations—specifically, what white adults expect and demand of white girls and young women. Instead of the fault line in Meghan's consciousness being produced by her needing to somehow ignore or not see all the ways our society has been and is structured by racism, here the fault line is a racial boundary that she was not supposed to cross. In other words, Meghan's story, in this reading, was about her being a young white woman who was suddenly close enough to a young Black man to become aware of his body. And in that moment of being close enough (or *too close* for white authority), she realized that the social fact that she was white and that Bob was Black mattered. Race mattered.

This second reading depends on paying attention to time and space as they play out in Meghan's story. According to Meghan, she and Bob had been friends since middle school. Furthermore, for Meghan, race or race difference had not mattered in this friendship before and she "hadn't really noticed he was Black until one day in high school." Thus, this story took up a particular moment in time within the context of a longer relationship.

It was also a story about a new space for their friendship. Meghan located their prior relationship in "middle school," which might signal not only that she and Bob were younger, but also that their friendship was *in school*. In her interview, Meghan told no other stories about, for example, interacting with Bob at their families' houses or at parties. If this was an in-school friendship, that means that they were usually under the surveillance of teachers, of white authority.

In the story, however, Meghan and Bob were in a new space—her car— and without adult supervision. They were two teenagers who knew each other, they were in a car (such a potent American symbol of freedom and forbidden love), and they were alone. Meghan noticed that Bob was sweaty. She noticed how he smelled. It was her closeness to Bob that allowed her to become aware of his body in a way that she hadn't before. And it was at exactly that moment of becoming aware of Bob's body, in a car, away from adults, that Meghan realized that race mattered.

Meghan had moved into what Thandeka (2001) called "nonwhite zones"—those psychic and interactional spaces that Thandeka thought were the

> killing fields of desire, the place where impulses to community with persons beyond the pale are slaughtered. . . . [where] the child develops an antipathy toward its own forbidden feelings and to the persons who are objects of these forbidden desires: the racial other. (p. 24)

When Meghan noticed Bob's body, she knew that race mattered. And when she knew that race mattered, she retreated from Bob: "And—and—and that was the only time."

There was no direct evidence, in her story or in other parts of her interviews, that Meghan had experienced the sorts of punishments for crossing racial lines that Deliovsky (2010) documented. However, as Meghan said, "that was the only time." At the time of the interview, Meghan was married to a white man. She reported that her family made "inappropriate racial comments" when she was growing up. It's not hard to imagine that Meghan would have already internalized, as a young white woman, prohibitions against being close to and alone with a young Black man.

If the above is plausible, then we can re-read the somewhat puzzling movement across different discourses of race difference that characterized our first reading of Meghan's story. That is, that she began with colorblind-ness, then moved to essentialist racism discourse in the middle, and then ended up back with colorblindness. But what if we interpret her words as being, actually, about space, about position, about the *distance between bod-*

*ies*—so that what we called colorblindness was actually a way for Meghan to express being farther away from Bob (and dependent on sight); that what we labeled an essentialist racism discourse expressed being close to Bob (and dependent on smell); and that what we again called colorblindness, at the end, suggested that Meghan was no longer close to Bob, that she had moved away (and stayed away).

We think that such an analysis accounts better for what, in the first reading, did not make much sense—when Meghan said, near the end, "And—and—and that was the only time." We suggested that she was claiming that this was the only time that she noticed race difference, but then that means, more or less, that she just chose to forget what was for her a rather dramatic discovery—an essential difference in Black and white people's skins and smells. Meghan said: "Then, still to this day, I don't notice that much of a difference. And I don't know if that's a good thing or a bad thing. But so far, it's worked for me."

However, our second reading emphasizes that this is not primarily a story about discovering racial difference, but a story about being close to and far away from a young Black man's body. In this reading, Meghan narrated knowing Bob as a friend, from a distance; then being in a car with Bob, being close enough to notice how he smelled; and then asserting that, basically, she never did that again, with Bob (or any other Black people). In other words, instead of interpreting "it's worked for me" as saying something like "this is what I think about race and it has worked for me," we instead interpret it as saying "I got close to a Black person once and I never did that again—and that's working for me." In this reading, the end of Meghan's story was not so much the re-assertion of colorblindness, but was instead her way of saying that she doesn't get close enough to Black people any more to notice any differences—and that this has worked for her.

## SO WHAT?

We were nervous about working with and interpreting Meghan's story. Even though we each have been talking and writing about race and whiteness for many years, this felt different. In part, we think that it was the linking of race and smell in Meghan's story that caused this nervousness, which in turn suggests that the white racial imaginary's fantasy about dirt is *alive and well*, despite (or nestled within) the dominant colorblind ideology of the current moment (Bonilla-Silva, 2001). In other words, we wouldn't have felt nervous if we didn't already know and feel this fantasy. Discussing Meghan's story put us in the position of repeating, of participating in, this dirty old racist fantasy, and our nervousness was caused, in part, by us being worried about being called or thought of as racists for participating in this repetition.[4]

However, we believe that our nervousness was also caused by the fact that work on whiteness and antiracism in education has too often been dominated by a *white privilege* framework, rooted in McIntosh's (1988) classic essay on privilege and the "invisible knapsack." Our Midwest Critical Whiteness Collective (see Lensmire et al., 2013) has explored and written about how this framework stifles nuanced explorations of race and white racial identity—stated over-simply, this is because, within this framework, the only work to be done is 1) to make sure white people confess their privilege and 2) to label as racists those who don't confess. In this chapter, we have been focused on neither of these tasks, which means we are vulnerable to accusations of not actually caring about the *real* (white privilege) work of antiracism.

For us, Meghan's story and our readings of it suggest at least two areas of crucial concern that need to be taken up in work on race with white future and practicing administrators and educators.

First, we note that, at the time of Bryan's interview with her in 2009, Meghan was a highly-educated person and perceived as a successful associate principal by colleagues and the larger white community. In her interview with Bryan, she expressed—and did not seem terribly self-conscious about it—a belief in the biological basis of race difference. Thus, while we might assume that, for white people in the United States, essentialist racism has given way to colorblindness, the current situation is better captured by Stuart Hall in his famous lecture, "Race: The floating signifier" (Media Education Foundation, 1997). Hall noted that "the biological, physiological, and genetic definition, having been shown out the front door, tends to slide around the veranda and back in through the window" (n.p.). The biological, physiological, and genetic definition of race is there in/for white people, whether expressed explicitly, as with Meghan, or not. Our experience in universities and professional development programs suggests that, too often, this definition of race is explored with white teachers and administrators for about as long as it takes to say, "It's not true." But why would we think that our assertion of this fact would somehow disable or wipe out centuries of racist thought and feeling?[5] We suspect that such non-pedagogy is shaped, in part, by the anxieties of white professors and activists that they not be seen as somehow repeating or participating in the old essentialist racism, but this avoidance just makes it easy for something like an "old" fantasy about dirt to "slide around the veranda and back in through the window."

Second, and especially in the context of vital efforts to help white women take up culturally relevant practices in their work as administrators and teachers in schools, more attention must be paid to all the ways that these white women have already been trained, through fear of being ostracized or punished by their white community, to *violate or resist* a key aspect of culturally relevant practices: The need to build bonds of respect and affection with, *the need to get close to*, the Othered children and families and communities with whom they work (Delpit, 2006).

In her classic *The Dreamkeepers* text on culturally relevant teaching, in a chapter called "We are family," Gloria Ladson-Billings (2009) argued that, for culturally relevant teachers, the "teacher-student relationship is fluid, humanely equitable, [and] extends to interactions beyond the classroom and into the community" (p. 60). This is a description of being among, of being close, bodily and emotionally. In contrast, the teacher-student relationship within what Ladson-Billings called "assimilationist" teaching is "fixed, tends to be hierarchical and limited to formal classroom roles" (p. 60). For us, this "assimilationist" relationship is, unfortunately, a description of where Meghan ended up in her story. After being close, after being with Bob in the car, she moved away from him, back into school and a formal relationship, far enough away that she claimed she no longer noticed race—and, unfortunately, this "worked" for her.

Decoteau Irby (2014) has recently published a brilliant and devastating article in *Educational Administration Quarterly*, in which he argued for the importance of using a "sexual fear/desire" lens to interpret the draconian disciplinary practices that Black boys are facing in our public schools. What such a lens helps us see is that "disciplining heterosexual Black boys represents a new campaign of institutionalized violence and intimidation that reflects a subtle, but nonetheless pernicious, White male segregationist agenda" (p. 785). While Irby correctly focused his attention in this article on how "young Black masculine bodies are disciplined through spectacles of harsh punishment and removal" (p. 786), he also explored how this segregationist agenda affected white girls, how "young White female bodies are disciplined through surveillance and coerced into compliance, conformity, and docility" (p. 786).

White administrators do not come to their professions empty, without experience. Meghan was a young white girl, once—along with other fairy tales, she learned a fantasy about dirt. Her lessons of difference were learned and reinforced by her white community. Meghan was once a white female teenager in a car with her friend, Bob, a Black male teenager—that would be the only time. Her proximity, closeness, to a Black body aroused a dissonance between her lessons of the past and her possibilities for the future. Distance became an intensifying signal for race. The closer and less supervised she was, the louder the echoes of the past became. Meghan is a white female administrator at a time in U.S. history when increasingly diverse school systems across the country are taking up a new disciplinary regime that targets young Black male bodies and that expresses an old white supremacist dream of racial purity. Her desire for distance amplifies these tendencies of segregation and undercuts the closeness necessary to develop meaningful relationships with students and families of color. Future research and antiracist pedagogies must pay much more attention to the intricacies of race, like the impact of proximity and its relationship to the legacy of racial segregation, in this country. Confession is not enough. We, as white people, must be willing to listen to our broken pasts *and* be willing to work closely together with people of color for a better future. As William Faulkner put it in *Requiem for a Nun*, "The past is never dead. It's not even past."

## REFERENCES

Bonilla-Silva, E. (2001). *White supremacy and racism in the post-civil rights era*. Boulder, CO: Lynne Rienner.

Davis, B. (2011). *A case study of how white high school administrators make meaning of their whiteness*. Unpublished doctoral dissertation. University of Wisconsin-Milwaukee.

Deliovsky, K. (2010). *White femininity: Race, gender & power*. Halifax and Winnipeg: Fernwood Publishing.

Delpit, L. (2006). *Other people's children: Cultural conflict in the classroom*. New York: New Press.

Frankenberg, R. (1993). *White women, race matters: The social construction of whiteness*. Minneapolis, MN: University of Minnesota.

Fields, K., & Fields, B. (2014). *Racecraft: The soul of inequality in American life*. London: Verso.

Gordon, A. (1997). *Ghostly matters: Haunting and the sociological imagination*. Minneapolis, MN: University of Minnesota.

Helms, J. E. (2007). *A race is a nice thing to have: A guide to being a white person or understanding the white persons in your life* (2nd ed.). Hanover, MA: Microtraining Associates.

Irby, D. (2014). Revealing racial purity ideology: Fear of Black-white intimacy as a framework for understanding school discipline in post-Brown schools. *Educational Administration Quarterly, 50*(5), 783-795.

Kovel, J. (1970). *White racism: A psychohistory*. New York: Pantheon.

Ladson-Billings, G. (2009). *The dreamkeepers: Successful teachers of African American children* (2nd ed.). San Francisco: Jossey-Bass.

Lensmire, T. (2011). Laughing white men. *Journal of Curriculum Theorizing, 27*(3), 102-116.

Lensmire, T.J., McManimon, S.K., Dockter Tierney, J.D., Lee-Nichols, M.E., Casey, Z.A., Lensmire, A., & Davis, B.M. (2013). McIntosh as synecdoche: How teacher education's focus on white privilege undermines antiracism. *Harvard Educational Review, 83*(3), 410-431.

McIntosh, P. (1988). White privilege and male privilege: A personal account of coming to see correspondences through work in women's studies (Working Paper 189). Wellesley, MA: Wellesley Center for Research on Women.

Media Education Foundation. (1997). Stuart Hall-Race, the floating signifier. Retrieved from www.mediaed.org/cgi-bin/commerce.cgi?preadd=action&key=407

National Center for Education Statistics. (2016, April). Trends in public and private school principal demographics and qualifications: 1987-88 to 2011-12. Retrieved from nces.ed.gov/pubs2016/2016189.pdf).

Omi, M., & Winant, H. (1986). *Racial formation in the United States: From the 1960s to the 1980s*. New York: Routledge and Kegan Paul.

Thandeka. (2001). *Learning to be white: Money, race, and God in America*. New York: Continuum.

# NOTES

1. For Frankenberg (1993), "discourses" refer to "historically constituted bodies of ideas providing conceptual frameworks for individuals, made material in the design and creation of institutions and shaping daily practices, interpersonal interactions, and social relations" (p. 265). Frankenberg drew on Omi and Winant (1986) in tracing the history of discourses on racial difference in the United States.

2. Thandeka (2001) traces the origins of white racial abuse against its own community back to the fears of white elites, at least since the beginning of slavery, that poor and working-class whites might align themselves with people of color rather than with their white superiors. Consequently, these elites have engaged in a series of maneuvers that divide and conquer common people, by granting limited standing and privilege to white folk while denying it to their Black sisters and brothers. For Thandeka, such actions by white elites produced, by the time of the Civil War, both an embracing of the idea of white supremacy by poor and working-class Whites and the reinforcement of the idea that some white people were better than other white people.

3. What makes it possible for Bob to be both *hypervisible*, as one of the only Black people around, and *invisible* at the same time is explored, with reference to Ellison's *Invisible Man*, by Avery Gordon (1997) in her *Ghostly Matters: Haunting and the Sociological Imagination*.

4. See Lensmire (2011) for an examination of both a "basement culture" in which white people continue talking in essentialist racist ways and how accusations of racism are used by white people in struggles for position in social hierarchies of worth and goodness.

5. Karen and Barbara Fields (2014) drive this point home with their discussion of how James D. Watson, "a Noble laureate for his work on DNA and founding director of the public Human Genome Project"—in other words, someone who should know better—reverted, during a 2007 book-promotion trip, to personal impressions and anecdotes in order to ignore all the scientific evidence and "prophesy that genetic evidence for black people's lesser intelligence would emerge within the decade" (p. 8).

*Chapter Six*

# Uneasy Racial "Experts": White Teachers and Antiracist Action

Zachary A. Casey and Shannon K. McManimon

We were stuck. The more we read, the more we talked, the greater the distance we saw between what was reflected in the academic literature on white practicing teachers and what we experienced around a circle of tables for three hours once a month with eight white teachers. Here was a group of teachers questioning their practices and identities and enacting concrete antiracist changes in their classrooms and schools. Yet they still felt uneasy and ambivalent about the work they were doing. Was it "right"? Was it enough? How should they respond to being asked to be an expert on race? Academic literatures had plenty to share about white teachers who were resistant to learning about antiracism—and there were also stories of successful antiracist work in classrooms and schools. But little helped us understand the paradox of doing the work while feeling completely inadequate.

This chapter draws on the two-plus years we spent working with eight white P-12 teachers from eight different school districts who were committed to getting smarter about race and racism, to how racism impacts our experiences as white people, and to antiracist responses and actions teachers could take in their schools and classrooms. We designed this professional development seminar for teachers based on historical, cultural, and social approaches to white racial identities and antiracism; we used both theoretical and practical tools that opened spaces for participants to move toward antiracist praxis: action and reflection in equal measure on their/our world(s) in order to transform it (Freire, 2000).

We facilitated this professional development seminar drawing on our own work as practitioners of antiracist pedagogies and practices in many educational spaces. In this chapter, we explore the uneasiness and discomfort three

77

teachers—Amelia, Morgan, and Veronica—felt about being positioned (particularly by their teacher-colleagues) as an antiracist or social justice "expert" precisely because of their work. We first share their stories and the antiracist work they did in their classrooms and schools. We then analyze their discomfort or ambivalence about their role as antiracist teachers. Drawing on conversations in our seminar and interview data, we position this uneasiness as stemming from three fears: fears of harming existing relationships, fears of getting it wrong, and fears of not doing enough. We maintain that acknowledging these fears, uneasiness, and trepidation—and sharing our own fear—is necessary for white people to work as antiracist educators. It also exposes the complicated and contradictory social location of whiteness(es), a multiplicity that can simultaneously lead to anger and defensiveness, to profound doubt, and to antiracist change. This dis-ease and ambivalence must be addressed as part of our responsibility in working with other white people in ways that lead to sustainable antiracist action and pedagogy.

## AMELIA, MORGAN, AND VERONICA'S STORIES: UNEASY RACIAL EXPERTS DOING THE WORK

### Amelia

Amelia is a chemistry teacher in a racially diverse, high-poverty, urban public high school. In our time together, Amelia often questioned her identity as a teacher; that is, she questioned who she was being in her classroom with and for her students. Part of her uncertainty stemmed from her struggles to explain how her school was racialized in the differently (and whitely) racialized social and cultural spaces from which she came and in which she lived. For instance, she felt a great need to "figure out who I am as a teacher, who my kids are. . . I feel like I need to justify to my family why I teach in a [large urban district]; they think my life is *Dangerous Minds*" (a movie in which a white woman becomes a teacher in an urban school working with students of color). For Amelia, communicating with her partner and other family members was important, but she feared she did not possess enough "factual knowledge" to have conversations about race in her all-white family. She asked, "If I can't even talk to my husband about this [systemic racism], how am I supposed to teach about it?" For much of our time together, Amelia remained the most unsure of all the teachers in our group regarding her own positionality and identity as a teacher.

Yet, in many ways, she was one of, if not the most, successful in developing and actualizing an antiracist action plan in her classroom and school. As a chemistry teacher, Amelia worked primarily with eleventh and twelfth grade students, and her course was required for students who wished to enroll in Advanced Placement (AP) Chemistry. After learning about and discussing the various ways that traditional classroom practices and procedures can work to reproduce racial injustice and talking with others in her building, Amelia examined her grade books to look for racial patterns. She discovered that African-American and Latinx students, overall, had lower grades in the homework category than white and Asian-American students; there were, however, no significant differences in their test and quiz scores. Amelia reasoned that if students showed on summative assessments that they understood the concepts and practices of chemistry, it was not as important for their course grade that they demonstrated these knowledges over and over on daily homework. She realized that she could separate homework (formative assessment) and quiz/test scores (summative assessment) and weight them according to her belief in their importance as assessments of student learning. If she did this, lessening the weight of homework for students' final grades, students' grades would more accurately reflect their chemistry knowledge as shown through summative assessments. She discussed these ideas with her students as she explained the new grading system and the ways she hoped it would be a better representation of what students were actually learning in class.

The results were striking. With less weight on homework, grades rose for many students—and students' motivation for continued success in the course also went up. As a result, in the second year of our work together, Amelia's school boasted the largest number of students of color in AP Chemistry in school history. Further, as other teachers in her department and building noticed her students' success, some also implemented similar grading practices. Amelia became positioned as a building leader around issues of diversity, specifically regarding helping more students of color succeed in challenging courses and advance to AP level coursework. This new positioning troubled Amelia greatly.

Her discomfort continued after the principal asked her to join the school's equity team, which leads two professional development days annually for the school. One spring, Amelia was asked to lead part of a session examining student data, such as test scores disaggregated by race and gender or data cycles from the school's various professional learning communities. Yet because the equity team was not responsible for pulling the data and was notified of this role at the last minute, this professional development proved difficult and ultimately not useful. She and other equity team members acted only as scribes, or, as Amelia said, we spent our time "writing down [other teachers'] noticings and wonderings from the data, not trying to infer anything. . . Our jobs weren't really to answer the questions." Examining data became nothing more than commenting on its format or presentation—not its meaning. Despite an emphasis on data at the school and district levels and Amelia's own results in using data to advance racial equity in her classroom, this schoolwide professional development led only to frustration as "no one can agree on what we want to do" and "nothing concrete has ever been decided" after examining data. This was further exacerbated because of a "major rift in the beliefs and the direction" of the equity team.

Amelia became more and more uncomfortable on the equity team because she repeatedly encountered resistance when she suggested books and articles—based on work in our monthly professional development seminar—that school staff might read together. Three figures stood out to Amelia: two women of color and one white woman. All three had been teaching in the school longer than Amelia, who was in her sixth and seventh years of teaching during our two years together, and all three resisted, according to Amelia, "anything that made it about what we [as teachers] could actually be doing." Instead, these teachers repeatedly employed culturally deficit orientations (see, e.g., Milner, 2006) to their students' home lives and cultures, suggesting that students' families did not value school or care enough about their children to help them be successful. Amelia was not prepared to encounter such resistance, particularly from colleagues of color. As these teachers were more "senior" than her, she felt that they were more "expert."

These kinds of interactions were on her mind when she was asked to lead in her building through equity team work. Amelia did not see herself as a leader, stating that "I think of an expert as being super confident, as someone who always has an answer, so I'm not an expert if I don't." Simultaneously, she knew that the questions of racial justice facing this and other schools have no simple answers. But due to experiences such as the poorly planned "data days" and conflict on the equity team, Amelia found that admitting to other teachers that she didn't have all the answers led only to frustration, as teachers in her building wanted solutions, not "to sit and talk and think for five hours." This was exacerbated by "the hypersensitive climate" in the building: teachers were hypervigilant—"on the defensive a lot"—about being called racist, particularly as the district had initiated conversations about reducing the high number of suspensions of students of color. Because of these tensions and fears, Amelia often found herself backing away from exploring difficult and time-consuming questions of what the school could be doing to create a more racially just experience for the majority of its students.

In an interview, Amelia said, "For me it's about locus of control: what do I have control over? That's what I can do." The experience with her equity team and with the senior teachers, coupled with teaching AP Chemistry for the first time during our second year together, produced a great sense of uncertainty not only about teaching, but about who she was as a person and what that meant to her. "I'm trying to figure out me, in my teaching, in my classroom, and I know others are trying too," she shared. Despite how her changed grading policies combated structural racism that had kept many students of color from enrolling in AP courses and that led to students' subsequent academic successes, Amelia remained uncertain about what was possible in her school and classroom. Her ambivalence hinged on her simultaneous feelings of longing to include more historically underrepresented students in advanced coursework and fears of alienation and inadequacy from her colleagues. These fears and vigilance remind us that our performances are also attempts to define our white selves in relationships to (white) elites; our performances, what we do and don't say and how we act, also enact our social relations. Morgan faced similar challenges in her elementary school.

## Morgan

Morgan was one of two elementary school teachers in the professional development seminar; for the past four years, she had been teaching fifth grade. Her school, in an immediate suburb of a major metropolitan city, was becoming increasingly racially diverse, now enrolling more than five times as many students of color as it had previously. These demographic shifts, coupled with her own learning in various spaces such as the professional development seminar, led Morgan to declare: "I see race everywhere now, in books, on the radio . . . but most other teachers [in my building] don't, or don't want to." Perhaps even more than Amelia, she struggled with how her colleagues positioned her and with the ways they dismissed her attempts to engage them in examining race and racism in practice in their demographically changing building.

With the support of her principal, Morgan was proactive in addressing race and racism in their school. Her colleagues, however, resisted her ideas for actions they could take at a building-wide level to address their school's racialized discipline and opportunity gaps. Frequently, Morgan attributed their dismissal to her positioning: she was teaching in the same elementary school she had attended as a student—making some of her former teachers now her colleagues. She shared further, "I look young, and I like to listen in groups. . . I just feel like they don't take me as seriously" as they do senior faculty. Yet Morgan set and enacted antiracist goals that positively impacted students, her classroom climate and curriculum, and the school.

For instance, in a seminar session, Morgan talked about a music teacher in her school "who is just old-school racist. He doesn't care to understand." Morgan noticed that this particularly affected one African-American student, Eric, whom the music teacher had labeled a "problem student." Yet Morgan believed that Eric was demonstrating "remarkable self-control" in the face of marked hostility. The music teacher frequently punished Eric and other students of color, rather than listening to them. To Morgan, it was very obvious that students of color were always those sitting in the hallway after being kicked out of class—and not just in this teacher's class, but in others as well. She wanted to figure out ways of supporting Eric and ways of interrogating why this pattern existed, even though she did not feel very hopeful that she could change the music teacher's attitudes and practices with students of color. Morgan realized that students *knew* that this teacher (among others) was punishing students of color; she began talking with her elementary school students about this. Morgan worked to provide emotional support for students by openly acknowledging with them how culture and power impact how we interact with each other.

This extended to academic work in her classroom, where Morgan engaged students in questioning the authenticity of historical texts. While some people might see such work as too advanced for fifth-grade students, Morgan's students had great success in these activities. They identified the lack of people of color as authors of or as subjects in their textbook and questioned why history focused on some groups more than others. This "consciousness raising" work, Morgan shared, felt closer to what she desired from her work with her colleagues. Morgan created a social studies curriculum based on interrogating history from multiple, critical viewpoints while also acting as an advocate for students of color.

Yet while she and her students learned through examining race and racism, Morgan experienced continued resistance and a lack of authentic engagement with the ideas and texts she presented to colleagues. For instance, because of racialized differences in which students were repeatedly sent out of classrooms, she asked that Delpit's (2006) *Other People's Children: Cultural Conflict in the Classroom* be required reading for the entire staff over summer break; her principal decided to make it optional. As a result, only about ten teachers read the book and participated in the subsequent discussion. This discussion, Morgan asserted, "totally failed. They kept saying things like, 'this was written in the 90s; it's too dated.'" Rather than discussing how such texts named the same racial issues present in their school, staff members avoided actual conversations about the texts' substance or relationship to their own school. While her students engaged in the kinds of critical reading she saw as cultivating more antiracist dispositions, her adult colleagues (all of whom were white) would not.

Morgan blamed herself for much of this failure, seeing her own whiteness and relative privilege as a part of why she could not "get her colleagues to understand, to really want to do something about it." Morgan's ambivalence, then, hinged on what she saw as her own complicity and failure to do *more* for her students: she personalized her school's failures as her own, and came to doubt her own ability to work as a change agent in her own school building, even though she was responsible for creating and leading the first group of teachers in her school's history that worked to explicitly address issues of racial equity and discrimination.

Early in our work together, Morgan was struck that her school did not have an equity team. While the other two teachers featured here worked in schools that were racially segregated (Amelia's school being around 90 percent students of color and Veronica's school being around 90 percent white students), Morgan's school was nearing 50 percent students of color. After almost two years of working with her principal and several other teachers, Morgan began an equity team for her school. Despite feeling like she wasn't doing enough, Morgan was raising issues of equity with students, in her classroom, and with colleagues.

## Veronica

Veronica, a social studies teacher in a distant suburban high school whose students are over 90 percent white, has become the teacher to whom others come with questions of "is this justice? Is this antiracist?" She has restructured curriculum in some of her classes yet recognizes that given the racial make-up of her school, "diversity" means something different than at schools such as Amelia's and Morgan's. The community sees the school as "high achieving," and many families take advantage of the state's open-enrollment policy to send their students to this school. "We've never not made AYP [Adequate Yearly Progress] as a school, so we don't have to do as much PD around testing," she told the group early in our time together. Veronica, more explicitly than any other participant, felt increasingly positioned as *the* expert in her school on social justice and antiracism. This positioning was troubling for Veronica, largely because of her own experiences and family background, which she saw as "totally different" from the kinds of social justice and antiracist work with which she sought to engage her colleagues. Veronica worried that she lacked "real experiences with people of color" because she had always taught in the same overwhelmingly white school and worked at a renowned European university in the summers, again with nearly all white people and students.

Veronica "grew up in a very conservative religious family. . . . I went to an all-white evangelical private school, a tiny school, and then to [a local Christian college]." At this undergraduate institution, Veronica said she "thought I was Republican, so I went to the first College Republican meeting, but I never went back." This early rupture began a pattern for Veronica, wherein she continually found through coursework in history and political science tensions between what she felt to be "right" and what she had learned growing up in school and from her family. In her masters degree program, she became even more engaged in antiracist work, citing a course on curriculum and instruction she took with Zac and a course on multicultural, gender-equitable social studies methods as the two courses that most impacted her "sense of what could happen in social studies classes" in terms of antiracist and socially just assignments and experiences.

Veronica felt at times like "an imposter" because despite her commitment to antiracism, she was not from a family that explicitly valued such beliefs and that instead accepted the status quo. Yet her critical reading of her district's Seeking Educational Equity and Diversity (SEED) group revealed her profound grasp of the limits of many approaches to antiracism and social justice with teachers. She described her experience of the SEED group in this way: "it seems like it's all about *moments*, people having moments and sharing those. . . . It's about experiences but not about changing things; the problem is always 'out there,' never in our classrooms or in our school." Despite these tensions, Veronica found it important to continue working with this group; they found her perspectives valuable as well, and she was asked to be one of her district's SEED leaders. While scheduling conflicts made her unavailable for this two-year position, the group has been trying a more action-oriented approach as Veronica had been suggesting.

In her own classroom, Veronica worked especially to redesign her world history course, which overemphasized Western civilization (partly due to expectations of vast coverage). She worked on this redesign in conjunction with updated social studies standards, attempting to "do more of the story that doesn't get told. . . more social history, and really challenging the dominant discourses." For Veronica, this was especially daunting in a course that was meant to cover the whole of human history from pre-historic times until today. Still, she shared that many of her students, by the second year of her redesign, were asking critical questions regarding how different peoples were positioned in history textbooks and working to deconstruct their own sense of U.S. exceptionalism as they engaged in studies of Western African kingdoms, South Asian trade routes, and South American religions and histories.

Outside her classroom, Veronica successfully cultivated a partnership with the urban school district closest to her school; she was one of the primary coordinators of a service-learning program in which students from her school (all white) paired with students from another school (almost all students of color) to travel by bus to another state to participate in building a new community center in a dispossessed community. She collaborated with teachers in both districts to combine SEED groups and participated in a special joint professional development session for teachers focusing on white privilege awareness and examining school-level policies that benefited white students at the expense of students of color. But, like Amelia and Morgan, despite these powerful practices of antiracist transformation, Veronica could not understand how she could be seen as an "expert" in her building on social justice and antiracism.

Near the end of the second year of our work together, Veronica shared, "I keep getting positioned as an expert, but I don't feel like one." She told a story about her building's peer[teacher]-coach coming to her "to ask about this Native American project for the sixth graders, and I told her which [one of the examples] I thought was more about social justice, but it's not like it's the only issue. . . . How can you view me as an expert?" Despite her numerous successes in creating opportunities for both her students and colleagues to engage in critical conversations about race, racism, and social justice as well as shifting from a focus on reflection and "moments" to more action-oriented projects, Veronica was unable to name herself as an "expert." Veronica's ambivalence was pronounced: she was able to create new collaborations and partnerships grounded in antiracist dispositions and clearly cultivated relationships wherein colleagues sought her help and support for their own work, yet her discomfort with her own background and positionality kept her from fully conceptualizing herself as competent in teaching about antiracism and social justice.

## UNEASY EXPERTS AS AMBIVALENT WHITENESS(ES) MARKED BY FEARS

These three teachers engaged in critical self-reflection and located spaces where they could work to transform oppressive practices and structures, creating more equitable conditions for students of color in their schools and districts and countering the whitewashing of curriculum. Our professional development work was in many ways what we had hoped: these teachers recognized concrete manifestations of white supremacy and discrimination and worked in material ways to combat them. Over two years, we supported each other in implementing antiracist actions and practices in classrooms and schools; we built a critical community, putting social justice theory into action.

Yet, as we talked at our last session about the future of this work, and when as researchers of this professional development we analyzed data, the uneasiness detailed above became, for us as facilitators/teachers, incredibly troubling. We had intended to support these teachers in naming for themselves the ways in which their schools and practices both limited and created possibilities for social transformation, and to support them as they took up positions of leadership in their various locales. We wanted our monthly Saturday morning professional development seminar to lead to something beyond our work together; we believed we were modeling ways in which a group of committed white people could come together to support one another and engage in the daunting yet inherently possible work of combating white supremacy in schools. A profound ambivalence seems to rest at the core of these teachers' experiences. We needed to understand this more.

When talking about race with white people, fear is often first positioned as fear *of* people of color. This form of fear views people of color, particularly men, as "dangerous" and prone to violence, as an attack on whiteness and white subjectivities (e.g., hooks, 1990; Jensen, 2005; Morrison, 1992). Second, white people fear being called racist. Both fears can limit action and understanding. Yet a much different fear, fear of being labeled an antiracist expert, has a comparable character: fearing rejection from other white people who don't share the same explicitly antiracist ideals can override sincere desires for racial justice and limit the actions and practices of antiracist white actors. This fear functions on the side of white domination, because it recenters white desires for acceptance and belonging at the expense of the concrete needs and experiences of people of color (e.g., Thandeka, 1999). Thus, perversely, fear of being called racist and fear of harming relationships with other white people can both stymie sincere antiracist efforts by white actors and directly contribute to the ongoing marginalization of people of color, both inside and outside of schools. Poring over interviews and conversations, we realized teachers engaging in antiracist practices had been expressing the following three fears: 1) fear of harming existing relationships; 2) fear of getting it wrong; and 3) fear of not doing enough.

### Fear of Harming Existing Relationships

In many ways, the worst thing to call a white person is "racist." Many white people, particularly those trying to redress historical acts of racism and bigotry, are profoundly afraid of being labeled racist. Further, due to the prevalence of colorblind discourses (e.g., Bonilla-Silva, 2003), many white people, including white teachers, see merely evoking race and racial difference as an inherently racist move: it is racist to call attention to race. In both Amelia's and Morgan's schools, fears of being called racist limited possibilities for action and for mobilizing (mostly white) teachers for antiracist practice. While both shared their own desires to avoid being labeled "racist," they also signaled a more general fear throughout their buildings from their white colleagues: the other teachers in their schools were afraid of being identified as "racist." But fear, in this case, went even further: these teachers also feared how other teachers and administrators would position them. Fears of creating antagonisms, and a more general desire for avoiding conflict, were central to the white character of teachers in our seminar. In our reading, these teachers had a deep-seated fear of the costs of antiracist work and the kinds of relationships that it would make possible—or impossible—among teachers.

Each of these three teachers had fears revolving around potential harm to relationships, particularly with other teachers. As Amelia struggled to define who she was as a teacher and person, she feared how other teachers whom she identified as more experienced (and thus, more "expert") would position her and her ideas for school-wide shifts in expectations and policy. She shared: "teachers in my school are afraid to refer any student of color [for discipline], because they think they'll be seen as racist." This led to avoidance of race, making Amelia unpopular for raising it again and again. For Morgan, fears over conflict with other teachers limited possible responses to the ways she saw teachers marginalizing students of color in her building. She did not know how to overcome their resistance without being even more marginalized herself. Slightly differently, Veronica's fears revolved around her limited experiences working with people of color: she feared this made her inadequate to the task of supporting others in creating more racially just experiences for their students.

Student-centered work requires that we decenter white teachers' needs for acceptance and belonging in favor of students' learning in powerful and political ways that enable them to question and engage their own lived experiences. Failure to do so, out of fear on the part of teachers, antiracist or not, works to (re)legitimate existing practices of racial domination and preserve the (oppressive) status quo.

## Fear of Getting It Wrong

Fears attached to losing closeness with others are directly connected to fears of "getting it wrong," of not doing "the right thing," to combat white supremacy as it manifests in our daily experiences. The current era of neoliberal accountability (see Ambrosio, 2013; Casey, 2016; Hursh, 2007) and teacher proofing (Crocco & Costigan, 2007; Sleeter, 2008) relies on "best practices." Given this common language, our insistence in this seminar that there are no best practices—in other words, no one practice or list of steps to follow that will *always* achieve our desired results—was deeply unsettling for many participants; it was both "very helpful and very frustrating," as Veronica wrote. "Teachers want the checklist," another participant told the group. This desire for a checklist of practices that would guarantee "good" antiracist outcomes speaks directly to fears of getting it wrong, of doing the wrong thing in living out commitments to antiracism. But given the complex, contextual, social, cultural, and historical nature of white supremacy and how it plays out in classrooms and schools, such a checklist does not and cannot exist.

Following the insights of critical educators, we insisted in our work together that we must, as teachers, resist notions of best practice because, as Kumashiro (2009) has warned, "no practice is always anti-oppressive" (p. 3). When we focus on one oppression or single out a particular discriminatory practice, we position other forms of oppression as less significant, as less worthy of response. Focusing on race and racism, in a culture and society that discriminates against women, queer people, and people who are poor, for instance, places more emphasis on one group of historically marginalized peoples than other. We must concede that our work to combat white supremacy may in fact function to support other forms of oppression. This is an inevitability; yet when we focus on fears of doing it wrong, we can forget that "there are as many brilliant forms of practice as there are brilliant practitioners" (Kincheloe, 2008, p. 116). That there is no *one* right way means that there are an unlimited number of possible pedagogical responses. This realization should fill us with hope and possibility.

Relatedly, as fallible humans, we will make mistakes in this work. That these mistakes can have serious negative effects on those most harmed by our oppressive reality is a felt struggle for the teachers featured here (and for us as educators as well). Their sincere desires to actualize their antiracist beliefs in their classrooms and schools limit their actions, as they fear doing the wrong thing (particularly in relationship to or in the conceptions of other adults) and (unintentionally) supporting existing oppressive practices. When these fears silence white actors, this silence functions on the side of white domination. Teachers must take up an engaged antiracist praxis, constantly questioning the ways they privilege or deprivilege others in everything they do. We know that white teachers (including ourselves) will get it "wrong" sometimes, but our pedagogical stance must account for such "failures" and provide meaningful opportunities for reflection and growth. Waiting until we know, for sure, that our practices will have the results we desire creates an impossibility: we will never know everything our students are experiencing in our schools or what the outcomes might be.

At the same time, we must continue our antiracist work. Fears of "doing it wrong" or "not knowing enough" too often stifle pedagogical stances of antiracist praxis. Instead, a more helpful approach might be to assume that we will always make mistakes—and thus always strive for ways and times to try again. These realities should not limit the scope and scale of our efforts, as there will always be more critical work to do.

## Fear of Not Doing Enough

Following from fears of "getting it wrong" are fears that our actions are too small, that we are not doing enough or everything we can to live out our commitments to antiracism. We can thus be ambivalent, simultaneously desiring to attempt change and ashamed that these attempts are not enough. White supremacy, as an overarching system of global domination, is bigger than any one white actor, bigger than any particular school, district, or even state. Thus, we attempted to make clear, in our professional development seminar sessions, that work in schools will never be enough, on its own, to bring an end to centuries of white domination. Yet, we insist on affirming the Freirean view of the possibility of schools to be part of such work, and further, that education is essential to such efforts, for as Freire (2006) wrote, "it is true that education is not the ultimate lever for social transformation, but without it transformation cannot occur" (p. 69). Combating racism in schools is bounded work. We are limited in terms of possible responses by the material realities of classrooms, schools, and communities, and the more we learn of the wildly dehumanizing structural and systemic forces that maintain privilege(s) and exclusion(s), the smaller and smaller schools and classrooms seem to become.

Amelia felt this limitation, and in her work to make sense of her positionality and possibilities for action, she insisted on naming her "locus of control" as the terrain upon which she had power and thus could make change. Still, despite transforming the racial makeup of AP science courses in her school, Amelia felt she was not doing enough, that there was more that she could be doing, even as she struggled to name what this "more" consisted of. Morgan shared repeatedly that other teachers in her building, in resisting the texts and ideas she presented, limited the possible reach of efforts to address the racialized discipline gap; she struggled with the various ways that teachers refused to take account of the home cultures of their students or forge meaningful connections to the communities the school served. Her work was not enough.

Positioned as *the* antiracist expert in her building, Veronica worried that others would not take up this work for themselves, as they needed affirmation from someone more knowledgeable to judge their work as acceptably socially just or not. Yet if antiracist work must first be approved by an outsider, it becomes difficult to imagine antiracist dispositions becoming part of the identity of teachers; antiracism then becomes merely another possible practice, another "option," rather than an attitudinal paradigm teachers and students bring to bear on anything and everything they encounter in their work together.

And, of course, these teachers are right: what we, and they, accomplished over our two years together is not enough. But how could it ever be? If we concede that schools exist within larger structures, work to transform only part of the larger structures will always feel incomplete. This is part of the powerful ideological workings of white supremacy, as fears of not doing enough can result in stasis: in not doing anything. That we will always have more work to do, that there is always more to be done, is again related to the Kumashiroan (2009) notion of the inability of any practice to always achieve its stated desired results. That there will always be more work to be done, however, must not be read as a totalizing theory of social reproduction, but rather as an invitation to carve out our own terrain, our own spheres of influence, in which we *can* act in pedagogical antiracist solidarity.

## CONCLUSION

To honor the work, thinking, and critical self-reflection that these teachers did and are doing, we must take seriously both their actions and their emotions. We must sit in the tension of expertise and uneasiness. They enacted antiracist practices, using skills and knowledge coming from training and experiences in our seminar and in their work and lives: they were experts. Yet engaging this expertise brought profound uneasiness and surfaced many fears. Reflecting on our work with Amelia, Morgan, Veronica, and the other seminar participants has led us to understand how a "both/and" pedagogical approach to whiteness was integral to any successes we individually or collectively realized.

In many ways, this both-and approach is analogous to the ways that we are conceiving of whiteness in this book and in our work. Whiteness is never singular and cannot be separated from individual and collective locations. As teachers, then, we recognize that a both-and conception of white racial identity, rather than an either-or binary, enables a more pedagogical and reflexive approach to antiracist work with white people. White people have *both* a "possessive investment in whiteness" (Lipsitz, 1995) that leads to white resistance and distancing strategies from complicity in white supremacy *and* powerful desires to combat inequality and past knowledge(s) in antiracist ways. Further, white people simultaneously long for closeness and acceptance from people of color and fear such proximity and intimacy. They/we fear that acting in antiracist solidarity will harm our existing relationships, particularly with other white people. For Thandeka (1999), such fears are central to what it means to be white: we are regularly forced to pick a side, and our desires for acceptance and love can often undermine our political desires for antiracism, for living out the antiracist beliefs we espouse.

The positionality of "antiracist expert" functions in much the same way. We simultaneously desire to enact meaningful antiracist changes in practice and discourse *and* fear the dangers of such work, knowing that we may get it wrong and that our efforts are miniscule in relation to the vast scale of white supremacy. The dangers of doing this work are real and are often expressed as fears of losing status, losing relationships, and even perhaps losing one's job. There are costs to engaging in antiracist work. While communities of color have known this for a long time, for many white people this is exceedingly difficult to realize.

As white teacher educators focusing on work with white teachers to combat white supremacy in schools, we too experience these ambivalences. For us, perhaps the most felt among these is the contradictory desire for participants to take up positions of leadership and act as building pedagogues to support other teachers in the work of antiracism alongside a simultaneous desire for humility on the part of white teachers. Here lies another paradox:

we are never and can never be finished with this work. Yet it is possible to engage in antiracist praxis without a finished or complete sense of an antiracist identity: we can be both expert and uneasy. If we credentialize antiracist dispositions, we evoke an illusory notion of completeness, of being "finished." We espouse a belief in teachers as lifelong learners, yet concomitantly, we desire teachers to be expert, to already know what to do. The idea of ambivalence is both hopeful and helpful in such moments. That it is both-and, rather than either-or, allows for pedagogical reflection and action, for praxis, on the part of white actors working for antiracism. Rather than working to resolve this contradiction in our professional development and teacher education classroom spaces, we would do better to name and exist in both spaces. Our participants made this clear to us, and their ongoing work to combat white supremacy, despite their trepidations, fills us with hope and possibility. White people can and must work to combat white supremacy in their daily experiences and practices, and such work does not have to wait for complete understanding or a final stamp of "gets it." We must learn to live with the both-and of white racial ambivalence, to teach powerfully from/in both positions, as we continue the always-unfinished work, of making the world and ourselves more fully human (Freire, 2000).

## REFERENCES

Ambrosio, J. (2013). Changing the subject: Neoliberalism and accountability in public education. *Educational Studies, 49*(4), 316-333.

Bonilla-Silva, E. (2003). *Racism without racists: Color-blind racism and the persistence of racial inequality in the United States.* Lanham, MD: Rowman & Littlefield Publishers.

Casey, Z. A. (2016). *A pedagogy of anticapitalist antiracism: Whiteness, neoliberalism, and resistance in education.* Albany, NY: SUNY Press.

Crocco, M. S., & Costigan, A. T. (2007). The narrowing of curriculum and pedagogy in the age of accountability: Urban educators speak out. *Urban Education, 42*(6), 512-535.

Delpit, L. (2006). *Other people's children: Cultural conflict in the classroom.* New York: New Press.

Freire, P. (2000). *Pedagogy of the oppressed.* New York: Continuum.

Freire, P. (2006). *Teachers as cultural workers: Letters to those who dare teach.* New York: Westview Press.

hooks, b. (1990). *Yearning: Race, gender, and cultural politics.* Boston, MA: South End Press.

Hursh, D. (2007). Assessing No Child Left Behind and the rise of neoliberal education policies. *American Educational Research Journal, 44*(3), 493-518.

Jensen, R. (2005). *The heart of whiteness: Confronting race, racism, and white privilege.* San Francisco, CA: City Lights.

Kincheloe, J. L. (2008). *Critical pedagogy primer.* New York: Peter Lang.

Kumashiro, K. K. (2009). *Against common sense: Teaching and learning toward social justice.* New York: Routledge.

Lipsitz, G. (1995). The possessive investment in Whiteness: Racialized social democracy and the "white" problem in American Studies. *American Quarterly, 47*(3), 369-387.

Milner, H. R. (2006). But good intentions are not enough: Theoretical and philosophical relevance in teaching students of color. In J. Landsman & C. W. Lewis (Eds.), *White teachers/ diverse classrooms: A guide to building inclusive schools, promoting high expectations, and eliminating racism* (pp. 79-90). Sterling, VA: Stylus.

Morrison, T. (1992). *Playing in the dark: Whiteness and the literary imagination.* New York: Vintage Books.

Sleeter, C. (2008). Equity, democracy, and neoliberal assaults on teacher education. *Teaching and Teacher Education, 24*(8), 1947-1957.

Thandeka. (1999). *Learning to be white: Money, race, and God in America.* New York: Continuum International Group.

*Conclusion*

# Who are We as White People to Be?: Thoughts on Learning, Loss, Confusion, and Commitment in Antiracist Work

Zachary A. Casey, with Shannon K. McManimon
and Christina Berchini

What do we want white people to do? We hear this question often: at academic conferences, workshops, panels, professional development seminars with teachers. . . "So, what do we want white people to do?" We answer this question, maybe too often. We describe additional readings, suggest looking into community organizations already engaged in antiracist projects, and so on. We act as though white supremacy, as a conditioning logic, as a totalizing system of dehumanization, is something that the white person asking the question might actually be able to act on.

Yet what happens when we conceptualize structural racism as something requiring particular actions that are already known, actions that a singular individuated social actor can undertake? This conceptualization makes antiracist praxis about information sharing. It assumes a fixed body of knowledge that has eluded those who have (apparently) been searching for; if they found it, they would know "what to do" about or in response to white supremacy. White supremacy is such a vast and multifaceted system of meanings, values, and oppressions that we must, indeed, aim to understand how all social actors are always-already enmeshed within systems of subordination and dehumanization. Yet, too often, white people's desires to know "what to do" place us as removed from or somehow outside of white supremacy—as if our actions might be "the answer." Instead of re-centering ourselves as white (savior) actors, we might ask: "what are we already doing?" And, "how do our routines and rituals respond to or reinforce white supremacy?" This is an ontological reorientation: moving from what we are doing, to who we are *being*, and to who we might become.

This is a very different kind of claim about what it means for white people to resist white supremacy and to act in antiracist ways in their/our social world(s). The chapters in this book seek to reveal the deep fissures, uncertainties, and confusions that undergird both our knowledge of what it means to be white, or to have a white racial identity, as well as the ways in which so often we, as white social actors, re-center our own privileges and complicity in oppressive systems. No white person, regardless of their antiracist credentials or past deeds, is immune from complicity in white supremacy. And thus, to respond to white supremacy as a white social actor, as a white person, means to respond to ourselves.

By responding to ourselves, we mean that white people need to understand the means by which they have become/are white; we must mobilize history and theory. The Reverend Harvey Johnson once wrote, "The white race cannot tell when they began to be known as such" (as cited in Roediger, 1998, p. 27). Many people today whom we consider "white" would have been considered a person of color at some point in U.S. history. While many peoples of color are unable to trace their specific family histories to other continents and the histories of people indigenous to the Americas have been deliberately decimated, today resources such as ancestry.com offer most white people a chance to understand (at least a part of) their family histories. Put into conversation with larger historical and social narratives, they provide opportunities to consider how their families *became* white. Such knowledge can help to destabilize the "normalcy" that accompanies so many white peoples' experiences of race and being racialized.

As important as this history is or can be, at the level of the personal, white social actors must interrogate the ways that their/our very ways of being and bodies themselves are at times complicit in white supremacy. There are moments, solely because of the body I am in, that I stand in for a host of dehumanizing and terrorizing moments in the lives of people of color when they encounter me. This is not because of specific, intentionally malicious things I've said or done, but rather because of what I represent in a particular social space. The work of Kevin Kumashiro can be instructive here.

Kumashiro (2002) has written about the ways in which we can better understand moments that feel oppressive. For him, oppression is citational: oppressive acts or instances don't stand alone, but reference our racialized past and present. To understand why a particular term or action is oppressive requires excavating its citational history: what it has meant, and for whom, in different moments in time. A white person in a position of authority over people of color, for instance, conjures moments wherein white people had a legal right to make explicitly race-based decisions on hiring and firing, home ownership, union membership, and more. This is why white people in positions of leadership in antiracist organizations, or in organizations with commitments to antiracism, are more than simply a problem of "optics"—as if the problem is merely how leadership appears and not what it represents citationally. This is also why many antiracist advocates have argued that intention is irrelevant in discerning whether or not a particular act or performance is "racist." Even if the offending party did not *mean* for their act to be read as on the side of white supremacy, if it feels that way to another, *it is racist.*

From such a stance, it might feel impossible to even imagine white antiracism. If white people are always-already complicit in systems of oppression and white supremacy, and if anyone who ever feels they are experiencing white supremacy from a white person is always-already correct in their pronouncement of racism, it would then seem that the risk of being called racist is the limit-condition of white antiracist activity. But at the same time, the risk—or more accurately, fear—of being called racist is a barrier to engaging in antiracist praxis.

Every white author in this book has been called racist. To engage in antiracist work, particularly as a white person, is to invite the entire history of white supremacist power structures into our daily lives in ways that many white people, because of their relative racial privilege, are often able to insulate themselves from. Most white people can choose when and if they want to think about race and racism, and the overriding desire for colorblindness, as Mary Lee-Nichols and Jessica Dockter Tierney detail in their chapter in this book, can often make white people respond to any and all discussions of race as always-already racist. It is racist to talk or think about race, so this logic goes, and thus the white person who studies race and who seeks to build momentum for antiracist activity is guilty of racism simply for thinking about race in the first place. If white people cannot stomach the accusation of being racist, because of their interest in understanding the ways race determines so much of our social reality, it becomes wholly impossible to engage in antiracism. Being called racist, paradoxical as it seems, is part of a commitment to engaging in white antiracism.

The desire to not seem racist responds to what, for many white people, is the worst possible racial epithet one might level at a white person. There is simply nothing worse, for a white person, than being called "a racist." Yet, if such a fear paralyzes us, it places us in a series of activities that actually *do* function to uphold white supremacy. Social norms in all- (or mostly) white spaces that call for white people to not mention race and racism function more to maintain our white supremacist status quo than most explicitly-racist actions or activities. In the words of Dr. Martin Luther King Jr.,

> I have almost reached the regrettable conclusion that the Negro's great stumbling block in his stride toward freedom is not the White Citizen's Counciler or the Ku Klux Klanner, but the white moderate, who is more devoted to "order" than to justice; who prefers a negative peace which is the absence of tension to a positive peace which is the presence of justice; who constantly says: "I agree with you in the goal you seek, but I cannot agree with your methods of direct action"; who paternalistically feels he can set the timetable for another man's freedom; who lives by the myth of time and who constantly advised the Negro to wait until a "more convenient season." (in Washington, 1986, p. 295)

If white people are not willing to endure a small slight to their character, how could they/we ever imagine being in solidarity with peoples who have been demeaned and belittled from their very earliest moments on this earth? If the fraction of a micro-aggression that is "being called racist as a white person" is enough to thwart efforts at antiracist movement building and solidarity, all hopes for a more fully human future are foreclosed.

This is why loss has been at the center of the chapters in this work. There are costs—emotional, social, and cultural—to participating in our white supremacist social reality, both for white people and people of color. This is not to conflate the dehumanization and suffering peoples of color face in white supremacy with the ways in which white peoples' desires for more authentic solidarities are thwarted in white supremacy. To be clear, no white person suffers *in the same ways* as people of color in white supremacy; this is what the history of white supremacy has ensured in the creation and maintenance of white racial privilege. However, that racialized groups are dehumanized in different ways does not mean that such dehumanization cannot function as a source of capacity building, as a place of coming to what South African scholar Jonathan Jansen (2009) has called "the recognition of likeness."

For Jansen, our pedagogical challenge in the wake of legal systems that protected white supremacy (Apartheid in his case) is finding ways to resist the overriding logics of juridical white supremacy that made any interracial solidarity and movement building an impossibility. This impossibility is produced largely through the citational oppressions discussed above, but is worth elaborating on further. If white people are called on to join antiracist struggles because of feelings of superiority—feeling bad for people of color, wanting to be seen as engaging in antiracism for the sake of face-saving, or actually internalizing a white savior logic that believes people of color need well-meaning white people to "save" them from other white people—their interventions function more to reinforce than to challenge white supremacy. In response, we can turn to what Jansen has written about brokenness as a way of orienting our white antiracism in ways that resist such superiority-enforcing antiracist interventions.

Jansen (2009) defines brokenness as "the idea that in our human state we are prone to failure and incompletion, and that as imperfect humans we constantly seek a higher order of living. Brokenness is the realization of imperfection" (p. 269). For Jansen, living in a white supremacist social reality breaks us—all of us—and our responses to this brokenness tend to position us differentially rather than in a shared relational capacity to work toward greater humanization. This means that the reason white people ought to engage in antiracism is actually not, *cannot*, be primarily about their/our conceptions of the present oppression of people of color. Instead, white antiracism should stem from the felt sense of brokenness that prevents the full realization of our humanity.

Such an approach to white antiracism gives support to the wisdom, shared by so many scholars of color, that the primary work of white people seeking antiracism ought to be in their/our own white communities, with other white people. And such work, most often, is the scene for the loss and confusion that this book stories and theorizes. We regularly confront loss in white antiracist work—loss of friendships, loss of respect, loss of opportunities—because of our antiracist work and commitments. But almost always, these losses are in relationship to other white people. As white people committed to antiracism, we must be willing to lose friends and run the risk of alienating others who are unable to read themselves ambivalently when we voice critiques and implement interventions on the side of racial justice. There are costs to engaging in counter-hegemonic work.

Yet too often, we encounter white people who desire to work against racism in ways that don't require any costs or sacrifices on their part, that don't require the confusion and messiness of this work. For these folks, white supremacy is understood as a dominating and dehumanizing global logic, but one that can seemingly be resisted through loving kindness alone. If we could simply respect one another, and treat one another with care, the ways in which white supremacy is reinforced in practice at institutional and structural levels would somehow disappear. This is naïve and counterproductive. Antiracism is not anti-meanness, and it certainly doesn't mean we ought to prioritize (white) cultural logics of politeness at the expense of acting in antiracist ways.

Thus, when we ask what we, as white people who seek a more just and antiracist social reality, should do, we should be prepared for experiences of loss in our excavation of who we are with and for others and how our ways of being work on and/or against white supremacy. We should also expect and understand the confusion at the core of such antiracist work on the part of white social actors. This confusion stems from recognizing that we as white people often simultaneously resist white supremacy as we re-center our own relative privilege. We can make strides in understanding our own complicity as we simultaneously alienate others around us. We can actively work to upturn racist systems and be read in such work as a stand-in for other white people who have belittled and demeaned our comrades of color in ways that prevent them from seeing all of *our* efforts as anything more than the same old racism. When such feelings are voiced, as much pain as it might cause for us, we would do best to listen—to learn as much as we possibly can from the interlocutor who has taken the extra step of creating a space wherein we might learn more about their experiences of us and our actions.

Thus, the central point is this: being called racist as a white person is an invitation to learn. While we will not always learn or take as much from every conversation about our complicity in white supremacy in ways that might make a positive difference immediately in the lives of people of color, this does not mean that learning is foreclosed in such moments. The worst thing we can do when confronted with our complicity in white supremacy is explain it away, by demeaning the person who has confronted us by delegitimizing their experience and telling them their understanding and experience are wrong: "That's not what, or how, we meant it." No. It doesn't matter. In such moments, our moral and political obligation is to listen, to learn as much as we can, and to respond in ways that signal our genuine commitment to more fully understanding the ways we can grow in our resistance to white supremacy, rather than hiding in the shadow of our relative privilege.

This work is never finished—and rarely easy. Yet there is no other option available to white social actors who recognize that their/our own humanity is bound to others in ways that subordinate and dehumanize so as to maintain a system that prevents any of us from realizing our full capacities as humans. We must act. And in our activity, we should expect loss and confusion. We must, as Tim Lensmire wrote in the introduction, expect dissatisfaction. We should expect defeats, and anger, and frustration, and being wrong, and making mistakes, and desiring to retreat or to hide. Yet in everything we do, we carry with us the profoundly human ability to build meaning from our experiences—to learn. And as unfinished and imperfect *beings*, our capacity to learn from our experiences and to learn with and from others—to *become*— remains our source of hope in ongoing struggles to live out our commitments to justice; to support others, both white folks and folks of color, to better articulate their own brokenness; and to fight for a solidarity that can and will bring forth a more fully human social reality.

## REFERENCES

Jansen, J. D. (2009). *Knowledge in the blood: Confronting race and the apartheid past*. Stanford, CA: Stanford University Press.
Kumashiro, K. K. (2002). *Troubling education: Queer activism and antioppressive pedagogy*. New York: RoutledgeFalmer.
Roediger, D. R. (Ed.). (1998). *Black on white: Black writers on what it means to be white*. New York: Schocken Books.

Washington, J. M. (Ed.). (1986). *A testament of hope: The essential writings and speeches of Martin Luther King Jr.* New York: HarperCollins.

# Afterword

## Beverly E. Cross

For this afterword, I have intentionally and purposefully chosen to write a letter—a near extinct form of communication—as the structure to respond to *Whiteness at the Table*. I have chosen to write a letter because I could not imagine responding to the powerful ideas in this book as a 140-character tweet, a snap, or an eighteen-minute talk. I want to think with the authors of the text and with the future readers as we collectively and individually reimagine educational practices using the compelling and complex ideas about whiteness that move beyond the trivial and dismissive references often evident in education literature. I am further inspired to write a letter in the spirit of Dr. Martin Luther King Jr. and James Baldwin who chose this art form to express, inspire, and lead justice discourse and action. Less than two weeks ago I was honored to actually hold one of Dr. King's original speeches in my hands. The typewritten speech included his handwritten notes in the margins and it ended with these words, "We shall overcome." Since then, I have been writing more conscientiously in letter form with my hand and with my mind focused on social justice.

Dear Authors and Readers Who Fight for Justice for Children and Youth,

I am finalizing this dialogue while sitting in downtown Memphis as it and the nation commemorate the 50th anniversary of the assassination of Dr. Martin King at the Lorraine Hotel just 3.4 miles from my home. Living in the midst of Dr. King's memories is a constant reminder of the power of a person, a people, and a movement. This living context gives special meaning not only to the historical moment but also to the times we now live in. The authors of *Whiteness at the Table* led me to think about the complexity and tensions of whiteness as *ideology, practice, and methodology*. I will play with these ideas as heuristic tools in the next few paragraphs.

My reading of *Whiteness at the Table* left me reflecting on its conceptual, epistemological, and ideological constitutive components. Theorizing about whiteness in these ways is significant to intensifying the conceptual analysis of the idea and examining the stories presented to illustrate whiteness in action, that is, as praxis. Through their stories the authors unveil a paradox in putting whiteness on the table. As they examine its operationalization by setting the table, they illustrate the necessity to simultaneously turn the place setting over to unmask the hidden pattern/mark of whiteness and its reflective capabilities to confront their own frustrations, heart breaks, and/or injuries. At the same time, however, examining their stories about whiteness as an act of equity paradoxically re-produces their privileged status, their hierarchy of power, and their positionalities to represent their identities, imagery, and social relationships while at times marginalizing others. They illustrate that examining whiteness as public analysis can both hide and unmask its oppressive capacities for themselves and others.

The authors apply and examine whiteness in very *practical* and contextual ways through stories of their lives as principals, teachers, parents, and academics. Their stories allow the authors to center their experiences as personal and societal examination of reality and to be thoughtful about the material dimensions of those realities to represent their world and to circulate it as truth. In doing so, they give us tools to view the operationalization of whiteness and white identities in daily silent ways and in powerful conscious ways. It makes transparent how they trouble their identities and challenges others to do the same through the ways in which they disrupt their unearned, uninvited privileged seats and positionality at the whiteness table.

I am intrigued how each author uses the power of storytelling to examine whiteness. At the same time, I am inspired to think of whiteness as not only a powerful concept and practical matter but also as a *methodological* paradigm: That is, whiteness as an ideology that can create methodological scholarly approaches that might lead to new epistemic ways of knowing. The authors attach their work to antiracist teaching, activism, and research about whiteness, and they do so as individuals and as a collective who are exploring methodologically how to challenge the concept, learn about it, confront the benefits of it in their own lives, and diminish its impact on their work and on others. What does it mean to center oneself, one's positionality, one's identity, and one's power in the struggle for justice for others and for society? I can imagine a new if not modified methodology evolving from the struggle involved in centering self and at the same time attempting to create a sense of solidarity toward equity and justice.

As I return to the beginning, I think about the struggle for justice continuing fifty years after the death of Dr. Martin Luther King. While *Whiteness at the Table* is not a direct response to this moment, it offers a significant marker in the power and injustices that still control the identities, realities, bodies, and consciousness of some while privileging others. It calls for whiteness to move beyond theory to practical analysis and critique. This represents some of the work yet to be achieved and presents a priority as we move into the next half century of the struggle for social justice.

In Justice for Children,
    Beverly Cross

# Index

# About the Authors

**Christina Berchini** is Assistant Professor at the University of Wisconsin Eau Claire. A native New Yorker from Brooklyn, she received her PhD in curriculum, instruction, and teacher education from Michigan State University. Her research on race won the 2016 Distinguished Dissertation in Teacher Education Award from the Association of Teacher Educators. Her writing on race has been published extensively in both academic journals and mainstream outlets. Her *Education Week Teacher* article, "Why Are All the Teachers White?", has been selected by SheKnows/BlogHer media as a 2016 Voices of the Year Honoree, and her Diverse Issues in Higher Education article, "We Don't Have a 'Diversity' Problem in Education," has been selected by SheKnows/BlogHer media as a 2017 Voices of the Year Honoree. Her scholarship centers on Critical Whiteness Studies and has appeared in the *Journal of Teacher Education*, the *Journal of Adolescent & Adult Literacy*, *English Education*, the *International Journal of Critical Pedagogy*, and other scholarly venues.

**Zachary A. Casey** is Assistant Professor of Educational Studies at Rhodes College in Memphis, Tennessee. His research and teaching focus on the intersections of critical whiteness studies and critical pedagogy. Focusing in particular on the ways in which neoliberal capitalism undermines antiracist praxis and pedagogies, his scholarship seeks to better understand the ways that white racial identity impacts possibilities for a more humanizing and liberatory education. His work focuses on building critical racial literacy and antiracist pedagogies with practicing and future teachers, as well as the social, cultural, and philosophical contexts of education.

**Dr. Beverly Cross** is the Lillian and Morrie Moss Chair of Excellence in Urban Education at the University of Memphis. She provides leadership in the College of Education's mission to enhance educational success for urban learners. Cross is nationally recognized for her record of teaching, research, scholarship, and service in urban education. She has conducted research in the areas of teacher diversity, urban education, multicultural and antiracist education, and curriculum theory, and she has written frequently on urban education, particularly on issues of race, class, and culture in urban schools and achievement. Her research has appeared in such publications as the *Theory into Practice, Journal of Curriculum and Supervision, Education Leadership,* the *International Journal of Educational Reform,* and the *Urban Review.*

**Bryan M. Davis** is the Superintendent of Schools for the Shorewood School District in Shorewood, Wisconsin. He has served over twenty years in public education in the state of Wisconsin as a teacher, principal, and superintendent. His research interests include urban education and the influence of race on school environments. He completed his dissertation, titled "A Case Study of How White High School Administrators Make Meaning of Their Whiteness," in 2011 at the University of Wisconsin-Milwaukee. His academic writing with the Midwest Critical Whiteness Collective focuses on how school administrators can improve leadership through developing a critical perspective of race in their school environments. He was a contributing author for "McIntosh as Synecdoche: How Teacher Education's Focus on White Privilege Undermines Antiracism," published in *Harvard Educational Review.* His chapter, "White High School Administrators as Racial Advisors," appears in the book *Perspectives on Diversity, Equity, and Social Justice in Educational Leadership* edited by Ashraf Esmail, Abul Pitre, and Antonette Aragon. Davis was nominated for the 2014 Wisconsin Superintendent of the Year Award.

**Decoteau J. Irby** is Assistant Professor at University of Illinois at Chicago in the Department of Educational Policy Studies. Dr. Irby's research explores equity-focused school leadership and organizational improvement. Specifically, he is interested in how adults make sense of and use their personal and collective influence and resources to transform educational spaces (including the self) to benefit Black children and youth's academic achievement and socio-emotional well-being across a range of K-12 educational settings. He is the author of over twenty peer-reviewed articles and book chapters and is co-editor of the book *Black Participatory Research: Power, Identity, and the Struggle for Justice in Education* published by Palgrave-MacMillan. He teaches classes on the topics of educational leadership, organizational change, and school improvement using methods grounded in action research, team-based inquiry, and active learning.

**Mary E. Lee-Nichols** is Associate Professor of Teacher Education at the University of Wisconsin–Superior, where her work is focused on preparing preservice teachers as anti-oppressive, antiracist educators. Her research examines educational policies and practices that continue to reproduce social inequalities in classrooms. She is especially interested in the experiences of white teachers committed to understanding the impact of this complex and imbalanced system on students and families of color in predominantly white, rural communities. In her current position she has advanced curriculum integration as an Act 31 Fellow through the University of Wisconsin-Green Bay First Nations Fusion Collaborative. She is a recipient of the Office of Multicultural Affairs Community Diversity Award, the Max H. Lavine Award for Scholarly Work, and the Making Excellence Inclusive Award.

**Audrey Lensmire** is Associate Professor of education at Augsburg University in Minneapolis, Minnesota, where she teaches elementary literacy methods courses and runs a civic literacy field experience at a local school. Dr. Lensmire is the director of the East African Student to Teacher Program (EAST) which supports future teachers of East African descent through scholarships and leadership development. She has published two books: *White Urban Teachers: Stories of Fear, Violence, and Desire* and, co-edited with Anna Schick, *(Re)narrating Teacher Identity: Telling Truths and Becoming Teachers.*

**Timothy J. Lensmire** is Professor in the Department of Curriculum and Instruction at the University of Minnesota, where he teaches courses in literacy, critical pedagogy, and race. His early work focused on how the teaching of writing might contribute to education for radical democracy and includes his books, *When Children Write* and *Powerful Writing/Responsible Teaching.* In his current work, Lensmire is attempting to re-imagine white people as racialized actors in U.S. schools and society, as part of the broader effort to mobilize white people for social justice work. His most recent book, *White Folks: Race and Identity in Rural America,* is grounded in the stories of eight people from a small rural community in Wisconsin—the community in which Lensmire was born and raised.

**Shannon K. McManimon** is Assistant Professor of educational studies at the State University of New York at New Paltz, where she teaches courses in educational foundations, multicultural and antioppressive education, and qualitative research methods for both formal and informal educators. Her research and teaching draw on her experiences not only in formal education, but on her work in nonprofits and informal learning. Largely using narrative, arts-based, and participatory methods, she studies the social and cultural contexts of innovative, equity-focused teaching and learning in content areas that include literacy, STEM, and professional development for educators. She completed her PhD in Culture and Teaching at the University of Minnesota.

**Dr. Erin T. Miller** is Assistant Professor in the Reading and Elementary Department at the University of North Carolina at Charlotte. She completed her PhD in Language and Literacy at the University of South Carolina in 2013. Dr. Miller's research is in the area of white identity construction, teacher education, and early literacy. Her ethnography of her young children's racialized identity construction won the American Educational Research Association's (AERA) Critical Perspectives on Early Childhood Special Interest Group's Outstanding Dissertation Award. Her work has been published in journals including *The New Educator*, *Ethnography and Education*, *The Urban Review*, *Early Years: An International Research Journal*, *The New Educator*, and *Journal of Curriculum Theorizing*. She is the 2017 recipient of the Social Justice in Education Award by National Council of Teachers of English's Early Childhood Assembly.

**Samuel Jaye Tanner, PhD**, is Assistant Professor of Literacy Education at Penn State Altoona. He is also graduate faculty in Curriculum and Instruction at Penn State's University Park campus. Sam's research concerns critical whiteness studies, arts-based educational research, and improvisation. Sam's first book, *Whiteness, Pedagogy, and Youth in America: Critical Whiteness Studies in the Classroom*, details a yearlong implementation of critical whiteness pedagogy with high school students. Sam also has a creative writing agenda that can be found on his website: https://www.samjtanner.com/

**Jessica Dockter Tierney, PhD**, is currently an independent scholar and stay-at-home-parent. Her scholarly work focuses on discourse in classroom spaces and examines how young people make meaning of race through laughter and other embodied forms of critical engagement. Her key publications, authored and co-authored, include "The Laughing Truth: Race, Humor, and Bakhtin in a Documentary Filmmaking Class" in *Knowledges Cultures*, "McIntosh as Synecdoche: How Teacher Education's Focus on White Privilege Undermines Antiracism" in *Harvard Educational Review*, and "Mobilizing Emotion in an Urban Classroom: Producing Identities and Transforming Signs in a Race-related Discussion" in *Linguistics and Education*. She also serves as an editor for the Annotated Bibliography of *Research in the Teaching of English*.

Made in the USA
Las Vegas, NV
12 April 2021